The fabulous land of

IRAN Colourful
and Vigorous
Folklore

The English texts are adapted in part mainly
from Iran today, edited by Jaean Hureau,
translated in English by Edward Burton, Edition
Jeune Afrique, Paris, 1975.
Historical Notes are taken from following books:
Islamic Architecture (Iran 1) edited by Antony Hutt and Leonard Harrow 1977,
Scorpion Publication London.
Persia edited by James Morris, Reger Wood, Denis Wright 1969, Thames and
Hudson Ltd. London.
Persia by L. Lockhart Thames and Hudson, London 1957.

The fabulous land of Iran

Compiled by: J. Yassavoli
Colour separation: Megaps, Farayand Gooya.

Lithography: Naqshafarin

Print house: Shadrang

Published in 2001 by Yassavoli Publications
Bazaarcheh Ketab, Enqelab Ave. 13146, Tehran, Iran.
Tel: (9821) 6461003 , 830415
Fax: (9821) 6411913 , 8832038
web site: www.yassavoliran.com

ISBN 964-306-016-0

CONTENTS

The fabulous land of

IRAN

Colourful
and Vigorous
Folklore

With over 340 photoes in colour

Compiled by

Javad Yassavoli

Photos by:

Nicol Faridani

Mahmoud Shahrabi,

Afshin Bakhtiar

Bahram Abedini,

Gholamhosain Arab

Mohammad Reza Baharnaz,

Sa'id Mahmoudi Aznaveh

Mahmoud Kouchakpour Kapourchali,

Ali Matin

Hamid Reza Hosainzadeh,

Asqar Adami

Abdollah Keyvani,

Abd-ol Khaleq Taheri

Afshin Alizadeh,

Asad Naqshbandi

Yadollah Valizadeh,

Mas'oud Zendehruh Kermani

Hosain Rahamni,

Fatemeh Ta'midi

Fars, Parishan lake ▶
Photo N. Faridani

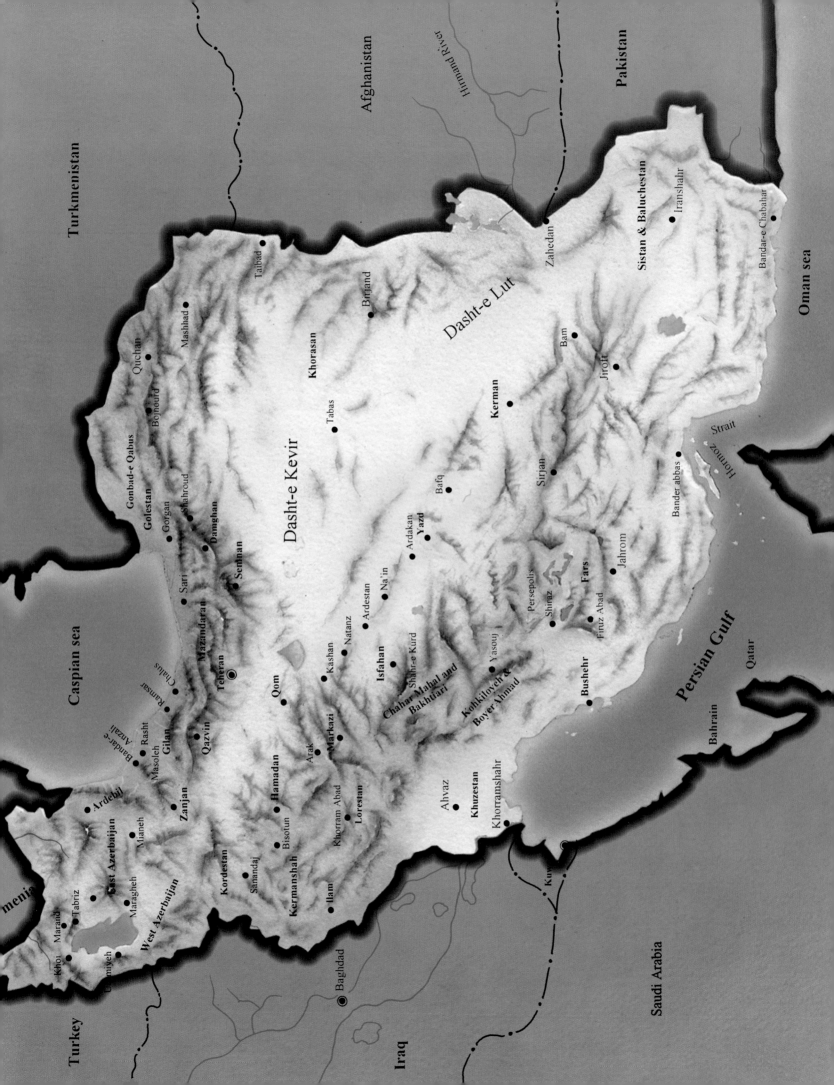

THE LAND AND ITS INHABITANTS

Immense Iran: 1,648,000 sq. km

The distance between Mount Ararat, on the Turkish — Armenian region — Iranian frontier and the south-eastern extremity of the country near the port of Chabahar on the Sea of Oman is longer than that between Paris and Athens. If Iran were to be superimposed upon a map of western Europe, the holy city of Mashhad would be over Budapest, Abadan within Sardinia, Tehran would take the place of Venice and Shiraz that of Naples!

The visitor must become accustomed to this scale of distance. This is important because upon it depends the planning of his trip and part of his enjoyment. Laps are always long. Excursions around a central point rarely take less than one full day. Persepolis, for example, considered as being "near" Shiraz is 60 km away and Pasargadae 130 km!

Every day a little closer

If you look at a globe, you will see that the north of Iran is on a level with Ankara, Athens or Lisbon, while the south is on the same parallel as Aswan or Tamanrasset in southern Algeria. That is to say very near the Tropic of Cancer. In terms of longitude, Tehran lies on a meridian 10° east of Moscow.

Iraq, Syria and Lebanon lie between Iran and the Mediterranean; but these countries, with names familiar to European ears, as well as Turkey, which is only partially Asian, the Caucasus mountain range which is a frontier between continents, are as many links between Iran and Europe.

The country has many specific features of its own in its landscapes, inhabitants, in its arts and customs. It has striking "picturesque" aspects. But over and above this superficial image, the enchantment of a visit to Iran is the feeling of contact with a "different", but not incomprehensible world, with a country which is both accessible, unusual and diverse.

Peaks, pure air and limpid skies

Altitudes, for example, are astonishingly high. One always refers to the Iranian "plateau", but not as an inhabitant of Sussex or Westphalia understands it... In Iran, Tehran climbs from 1,200 to 1,700 metres; Hamadan is at 1,820 metres; Kermanshah at 1,630; Shiraz at 1,600; Isfahan at 1,430; Zahedan, Tabriz and a dozen other cities at 1,400 metres...

The term "high plateau"-invented by geographers- is a confusing one. The Iranian plateau is not a flat table, an endless erg. There is always a mountain range on the horizon with some strange profile: cliffs with tortuous strata, ribbed, embattled and cracked towers, chipped needles, well-worn domes. Frequently there is no transition: an impassable mountain range suddenly juts out of a plain; the road runs along the foot of a wall of rock over long distances. Large mountain ranges slice the country into sections.

In the north, the Alborz (Elburz) range forms a Continuous wall above the Caspian coastline. Only three roads make their way through it, with difficulty. Its Highest point is the inactive Damavand volcano, whose Snow-covered peak is at 5,671 metres, 850metres higher than Mount Blanc! Several other peaks exceed 4,000 metres. Mount Tuchal, near Tehran, is close to that altitude. To the north-west, the Alborz range is linked by an intricate complex to the Azerbaijan mountains overlooked just beyond the Turkish frontier by the famous Mount Ararat where Noah's Ark was reputedly stranded. Its height exceeds5,000 metres. To the east, the Alborz range runs into the Khorasan mountains which are less high and more accessible.

The western part of Iran is streaked by parallel Ranges, maybe less impressive than the Alborz range, but even less easy to cross. They make up the Zagros range, with peaks between 4,000 and 4,500 metres, but so laid out that no road can be built through them.

Along the Persian Gulf and the Sea of Oman, Parallel ranges form a series of barriers rising higher and higher up to the edge of the Great Desert. The soaring landscape, spectacular when seen from a plane, is not conducive to easy penetration but, little by little, modern roads are making their way through it.

Parallel to the Zagros mountains, another range runs along a distance of 1,000 kilometres from Zanjan to the Kerman region. In Numerous volcanoes, now extinct, make its structure more complicated. Most of them exceed 4,000 metres.

In the center of these ranges, maps show a big empty white space. Its northern portion is the Dasht-e Kavir, a former salt-lake, a desert of stones, sand and salt, and the southern portion is the Dasht-e Lut, a practically inaccessible ocean of sand. These two deserts cover about one third of the country. Since Iran is three times larger than France, the desert alone is as large as that country.

Predominant shade: a delicate fawn
The colour of Iranian landscapes is one of the attractions, may be the major attraction, of a trip through the high plateau. One gets used to the tortured uneven ground, but one never tires of the subtly-changing hues of the deserts and mountains. From one slope to another, from one valley to another, ochres, reds, greens follow each other or mingle, stretching across the whole of the horizon or super-imposed on the flank of a same cliff. There is suddenly a pure white pyramid or an almost jet-black peak standing out against the deep blue sky.
But the predominant shade is a delicate fawn similar to that of a young deer's skin. This impression is accentuated by the composition of the soil. Where there are no cliffs or rocky slopes, hills and mountains have a velvety appearance: they are covered by impalpably fine sand which softens contours and absorbs shadows. When the wind blows, large brown scarves of swept sand rise above the mountains, twist and turn above the plain and come down upon villages steeped in the same colour.
Due to the high altitude of the plateau, few trees grow spontaneously, few species can subsist in the intense cold of the continental winter.

Poplar oases gracing the high plateau
The poplar is the typical Iranian tree. Its frail silhouette, its sparkling leaves and silvery trunk are part of the Iranian landscape. In tight clusters or in straight lines around gardens, poplars provide pleasant greenery in the highland countryside. They also provide a precious material: wood which is used as

Anzali Lagoon, north of Iran ▶
Photo N. Faridani

10

timber for cob houses, handles for farm implements, bridges over streams, shafts for carts and carriages and flag-masts for celebration. It is never used for heating, now increasingly based on national petroleum supplies.

The smallest village is surrounded by poplar-trees, the smallest trickle of water is lined with them. The term "poplar oasis", currently used in Iran, may come as a surprise to visitors. But it is quite appropriate. An oasis is a small islet of vegetation enjoying the shadow of a few trees and lost in a mineral ocean. This is an exact definition of many towns and villages in the high plateau. The poplar simply replaces the date-palm found in Saharian or Arabic oases: Both types of oases provide a striking example of a community struggling against hostile natural surroundings, out of which man's ingenuity manages to derive a precarious living.

And from the somewhat egotistical viewpoint of the foreign visitor, the enchanting contrast between aridity and cool shade, parched soil and tender greenery remains.

A score of large modern dams

Water is a vital problem. Snow falls on the high mountains and rain is plentiful in the north and west of the country. But you can cover hundreds of kilometres without crossing a river worthy of that name. Only one, the Karun river, which comes down from the Zagros range, receives the waters of the Arvand-rud, then flows into the Persian Gulf near Abadan, is navigable during part of the year. In the north, the Qezel Owzan river which has its source at Sanandaj and carries its waters to the Sefid-rud, is the only torrent of some importance. There are also two rivers forming the northern frontier, the Atrak to the east and the Aras to the west. All the others run tumultuous waters for a few days when the snows melt or a few

hours after a storm and then disappear into the desert sands. The sun and the scorching north-east wind rapidly vaporate the water which accumulates in depressions indicated on maps by blue dotted lines and visible from a plane because of the silver and delicate pink colour of the soil.

In the north-east of the country, most of the water flows into the immense Urumiyeh Lake and is lost for consumption since the inland sea is so saturated by mineral salts that even fish cannot live in it.

Under these circumstances, how can oases become green, without rivers or sources? How are they supplied with water? By what miracle do pastures, gardens and orchards prosper in the midst of arid zones? Very often there is no transition whatsoever between sand and rock and salad fields or clusters of poplar-trees. On one side of a road, you find desert land, on the other rich greenery.

There are two answers to this, two techniques, one recent and the other as old as mankind.

The Iranian State recently launched a major dam-construction program: nineteen large projects and a series of lesser ones. These achievements are all the more remarkable since the reservoirs are frequently located in remote places far from building material supply centres. As the implementation of the program progresses, the production of electric power, water supplies for cities and irrigation possibilities are considerably improved.

At the same time, deep drillings are being carried out and equipped with pumping devices. The water is distributed locally through canals, or under pressure, through pipes.

This is not a new problem. King Shapur I, in the 3rd century, held captive Roman engineers to build bridge-dams with mobile locks. There are still visible vestiges of these (particularly at Paipol, near Susa).

During the 14th century, the Iranians invented the vault-dam (there is a specimen to the south of Qom).

During the 17th century, they built the Khwaju Bridge in Isfahan which regularizes the flow of the Zayandeh-rud river.

"Qanats" illustrate age-old ingenuity

Hundreds of villages subsist thanks to a much older technique than that of large dams: the "qanats".

It is not known whether the system was devised during the reign of Cyrus the Great or before his time.

Although two thousand five hundred years old, or even more, it still performs its functions. Specialists from the United Nations Food and Agriculture Organization(FAO) and engineer-agronomists from arid land countries come to study this technique. This proves that it is still valid today. They carry out experiments in areas which are sterile for lack of water. In Iran itself, the "qanats" are maintained, sometimes at great cost to communities, and some new ones are dug.

A qanat is an underground ditch sometimes more than one hundred kilometres in length and ten, twenty or thirty metres deep. Some are reputedly up to fifty metres deep. The qanat usually starts at the foot of a mountain and ends up in a village, an oasis or even a single house. Its presence is noticeable at surface level by an alignment of molehill-like humps.

The Persian Gulf and Sea of Oman

Only suitable for a winter sojourn, this seaside area is marvellous. The vegetation is stunted and scanty but untouched natural landscapes stretch out under permanent sunshine.

There are only a few recreation and holiday centres. They are in the Bandar Abbas area and in the is lands nearby, but Iranians in Tehran are already referring to their "Riviera" and the hotels are frequently full.

Unfortunately, from May to October climatic conditions are far from comfortable. Torrid heat and humidity rising from the estuaries and lagoons are difficult to bear..

Nevertheless, intense activity takes place in several spots along this huge coastline. Since 1972, many port, industrial, military and social facilities have been setup.

Modern roads tie in to ports which are egaining their historical predominance.

Bandar Abbas, which commands the Hormoz Straits, has doubled its population; two new deep-sea ports have been built there. Jask, which hardly features on maps, will be Bandar Abbas's counterpart on the Sea of Oman. The same will soon apply to Bandar Lengeh, a port which lies at the mouth of the Gulf; Iran-Air planes stop off there regularly.

Further to the north, Bushehr is experiencing a revival of activity now that it is no longer by-passed by the roads to Shiraz and Ahvaz.

Studded along the bottom of the Gulf, the ports of Khoramshahr, Abadan, Bandar Imam and Mahshahr are devoted to the petroleum divinity while in tribute to its omnipotence, Khark operates installations which are unique in the world.

The Caspian coastline is quite another story. Few of the preceding observations apply to the thin strips of territory which make up the Iranian provinces of Gilan, Mazandaran and Gorgan. It runs from Astara, on the frontier with the Republic of Azerbaijan to Bandar Turkman near the frontier with the Republic of Turkmenistan.

The Caspian coast: 630 km of greenery

In contrast with many parts of Iran where one lives at altitudes up to 2,000 metres, the level here is — 20 metres. In the rest of Iran the air is dry, limpid; clouds are rare and appear as mere decorations. Here on the contrary your skin and lungs recapture a forgotten flexibility.

The sky is often covered by thick clouds which come and burst on the neighbouring mountains.

At Rasht, the annual rainfall is 1.30 metre. There is no need for "qanats", there is enough water for 355,000 hectares of rice paddies and for about the same surface of cotton fields. Wheat, barley, sugar-cane, and tea seem to take pleasure in growing in this region where the balance between sunshine and rain seems orchestrated by some divinity. Timber which is so rare a material on the plateau, is of current use here. Wood fences surround pastures where horses prance and fat cattle graze. Houses and granaries are made of logs, beams and boards (when not of concrete); most of them are raised from the ground on piles to protect them from the humidity of the soil. Thick forests of difficult access cover the abrupt slopes of the Alborz mountains.

The peaks of these mountains are sometimes only just over a kilometre from the coast. Torrents have dug deep ravines where only hunters dare to venture.

Torrents widen and become calm as they go through the plain and form large estuaries enjoyed by fishermen, washerwomen, children and ducks... Sturgeons hide in these estuaries since they are usually fished out at sea. And, of course, there is the beach. A really long beach, almost unending. In some places the sand is light-coloured and very fine, in others it is grey and mixed with gravel and crushed sea-shells. Perched on sand-dunes, a few metres high, villas, new housing developments and holiday villages dotted along the central portion of the coast overlook the sea.

Under trees behind the sand-dunes, camping and picnic sites have been organized.

Restaurants and motels have been opened every so often. And there are even two or three international-class resorts with first-class hotels:

Babolsar, Ramsar, Lasht-e Neshar. There should be some coordination in the development of these facilities, most of which are recent. There should also be regulations to protect this coastline, an exceptional high spot of Iranian tourism, from the confused proliferation of villas with ostentatious colours and of varying styles.

This would certainly not prevent the Caspian coastline from remaining the principal seaside resort and a fashionable centre for thousands of inhabitants of Tehran.

Ostans, shahrestans and farmandaris

There are different names for the administrative regions of the country. The "ostan" is a province; a governor-general represents the central government.

The "shahrestan", a sub-division of the ostan, is equivalent to a "county". It is headed by a governor.

A "farmandari" is a kind of district which enjoys a certain degree of administrative autonomy.

A few sectors of tourist expansion cover several provinces. As we saw earlier, this applies to the Caspian coastline. Elsewhere, the administrative entity usually corresponds to a territory having some sort of geographic and ethnic unity. This is the case for Kurdestan and also for Azerbaijan (while admittedly there are an eastern and a western Azerbaijan).

Conversely, it happens that some very large provinces are only partially visited by foreigners. For example the Khorasan province administratively includes the Kavir Lut or Great Desert area which are obviously not very accessible but it also comprises jewels like Mashhad in the north.

The structures and administration of Iran is that of a modern country. The Nation is unified. The Farsi (or Persian) language is the national language, taught in schools throughout the country.

The population of Iran is made up of several

◄ Persian Gulf, south of Iran,

15

ethnic groups. A majority of these belongs to the great Indo-European family, others emigrated from Central Asia or settled during the Muslim conquest; in the case of some, such as the Lors and the Kurds, the origin of their settlement is too ancient to be determined. Foreign visitors, even when not forewarned, cannot fail to note this ethnic diversity reflected in dress, folklore and the shape and decoration of houses.

In north-eastern Iran the Turkmans originally came from the steppes. They became sedentary a generation or two ago and the steppes gave way to the cultivation of cereals. But the tradition of nomadism is still deeply rooted. You meet bearded shepherds wrapped in felt cloaks with their astrakhan toques pushed down to their slanted eyes. And these men from the steppes are naturally horsemen. Horse markets are the main event of the week. The one held in Aq Qala, near Gorgan is easily accessible to tourists. (It is usually held on Thursday). The women wear red scarves and silver jewels. Round "yourt" dwellings, with woven reed walls and skin or felt roofs are to be found, next to the recently constructed concrete square houses with wooden peristyles.

At the centre of the eastern frontier, dark-skinned Seyyed fishermen and livestock-breeders live in semi-lacustrian villages. They move around in the labyrinth of marshes and lakes in the Sistan region (near Zabol) on boats made of reeds.

The whole southern and south-eastern portion of Iran was only yesterday still run on a nomad-type economy.

In all areas where annual rainfall does not exceed 250 mm, nomadism in search of pastures is a necessity imposed by nature which only intensive irrigation and industrialization can change.

In Iran today, irrigation, and industrialization are priority matters. For this reason; the Baluchi, for example, lead less and less

semi-nomadic lives. They are rapidly adapting themselves to sedentary jobs created as a result of development projects and are settling in permanent housing in rebuilt districts of Bandar-e Abbas, as just one striking example of this kind of transformation.

The same phenomenon applies to the Qashqais from the Fars mountains. They settle, at least temporarily, in small towns and even in Shiraz where men work in the bazaar and women become maids. One is then free to admire their scarlet robes but photographing them would not be well taken unless you obtain prior permission from their husband or parents.

Colourful and vigorous folklore

The Bakhtiaris usually live in inaccessible valleys in the Zagros mountains. In winter they go down to the Khuzestan and Lorestan plains where each year a larger number of them settle, attracted by new agricultural developments in this region affected by several large irrigation projects. Otherwise they lead a secluded and peaceful life in their black goat-hair tents.

Kurdestan lies in the west and north-west. In point of fact, most of the Iranian Kurds are settled in towns, sometimes large ones (Sanandaj, Kermanshah, Saqqez, Urumiyeh, etc.) and entertain very friendly relations with foreign visitors. The main problem is to find an interpreter since most of them speak their ancestral language. They are perfectly amenable to being photographed. They are handsome men whose dignity is underlined by their black dress: fringed turban, smocks worn tight around the waist, baggy trousers. Women and children prefer wool, cotton, and especially artificial silk dresses in crude bright colours: mauve, pink, orange, sometimes gold spangled.

Tolerance, a state rule

Azerbaijan, although mountainous, is a natural and millenary transit region. It is inhabited partly by Kurds, and by other groups: Turks,

Armenians, Assyrians. Its folklore is well preserved.

In addition to ethnic diversity there is a variety of religions. Around Esther's tomb at Hamadan, a Jewish colony settled in Babylonian times still lives there in full freedom. And it is not the only one.

The Zoroastrians who represent the astonishing survival of the early Aryans' faith, still perpetuate the teachings of Ahura Mazda and of the great philosopher Zoroaster. Several "Towers of Silence" are set on the peaks of mountains between Yazd and Kerman, a region unfortunately remote and of difficult access.

The Armenian church and fortified monastery of St Thaddeus in northern Azerbaijan are not only excellent goals for excursions but also a rallying-point for thousands of Christian pilgrims (in July). There are about two hundred thousand Armenians in Iran. Their biggest community is in the Jolfa district at Isfahan which has thirteen parishes, a cathedral and an "Asian Catholic Museum". Sunday mass at St Saviour Cathedral is an unexpected event in the heart of a Muslim nation.

Iran the nation of the Aryans

Though there is a certain diversity in the composition of the Iranian nation, the main group is of Persian (or more precisely Aryan) stock.

Originally, various peoples associated with the great "Indo-European" family occupied the Iranian plateau while pursuing their slow westward migration. Then, as history was dawning, a more homogeneous group, the Aryans, speaking a common language, having mastered horsemanship and using war chariots, appeared from the north-east, crossed the Oxus or Amou-Darya river and settled in Persia. The country of the Aryans became known as "Aryana" the origin of the name "Iran".

The heart of the Aryan country was the Fars ("Persia") region. Another group further north was made up of the Medes. It will be recalled that Cyrus's Empire was formed as a result of an alliance between the Medes and the Persians. This nucleus of the Persian nation was only slightly polluted by numerous and often dramatic invasions.

Visits to the cities of tomorrow

After the Islamic revolution, extraordinary changes are being carried out at an increasingly fast rate. The least well-informed visitor is able to see this for himself. Increasingly eloquent testimonies of a new Renaissance now supplement traditional tourist values: antique vestiges, monuments representing the great periods of artistic development and well-preserved crafts. Tourism in Iran has always centred upon its towns. And the attraction of these towns is enhanced by the interest provoked by the discovery of a nation in full progress, building its own future.

Naturally it is in the cities that the movement is the most noticeable. It is reflected by a proliferation of new buildings: factories, schools, universities, government offices, hospitals, hotels, etc. Open spaces are being cleared by town planners to improve the access to monuments, mosques and palaces. Flower-beds and fountains are appearing at cross-roads, gardens and parks are open to the public. At night, bridges, squares, castles and minarets are floodlit. Roads are being improved: boulevards, avenues and deviations are being built; new street-lighting is being installed and existing lighting improved.

Tehran, the capital, leads the pack in this race but all provincial towns are also participating in this movement.

Although most new buildings are purely utilitarian, this does not exclude aesthetic research. Harmonization with the surrounding landscape (based both on outline and colour), the use of traditional decorative materials (brick, ceramics), the choice of classical architectural motifs (cupolas, pointed arches, towers, etc.) often identify these new buildings as offshoots of the great periods of Iranian art. Recent regulations impose the observance of traditional styles. The Bandar Abbas Museum, the Kerman Technical School, the Shiraz Television Building are, among hundreds of others, an illustration of this trend.

And when this is not the case (there are unfortunately many soulless concrete and glass buildings), one must admit that houses built during the 19th century which make up the major part of most Iranian cities are even more dreary. Conversely, the architecture of certain commercial buildings such as, among others, banks have a somewhat bombastic appearance which is not devoid of picturesque aspects.

Having recognized the merits of modern Iran and admired its dynamism, the tourist is impatient to discover Iran's historical wealth, pictures of which haunted him long before he left for Iran: blue domes decorated with intricate arabesques, minarets with balconies and lantern-turrets which dart skywards in batteries of four, five and sometimes eight; the immense court-yards with apses at the four cardinal points; the deep and mysterious "iwans" with the luminous glaze of the mosaics reflecting all the blues in Paradise, and as dark as the doors of Hell.

Rigorously original monumental art
Mosques, (particularly the Friday Mosque, called "Masjid-e Jom'eh") are nearly always the most interesting monuments in the town, because they are frequently very large or because of the wealth and inventiveness of their decoration, the beauty of their setting and sometimes their historical background. But these are not the only centres of interest.

"Madrasahs" (Koranic schools) have, in addition to an architectural daringness and decorative style very similar to those of mosques of the same period: charming interior gardens around a central water pool in some cases circular and in others with a festooned contour.

The silent deambulation of theology students, dressed in long grey robes, with their immaculate turbans, their smiling conversations carried out in shady corners, without even raising their voices or disturbing the peaceful and secluded atmosphere, create an exquisite ambiance which the visitor has great difficulty in leaving.

Mausoleums are by far the most numerous interesting monuments in Iran. They were built to commemorate religious chiefs (Imams or Emams), holy priests who frequently were Imams' sons ("Imamzadeh": the name designates the person as well as the monument built in his honour), historical figures or poets, many of whom still enjoy popularity among the people.

The size of the monument and the richness of the decorations vary according to the fame of the defunct figure. The sanctuary built to commemorate the most venerated of them all, Imam Reza, at Mashhad where he was martyred, and those at Qom and Ray can be seen from afar by pilgrims and tourists alike because of their golden cupolas. They are towns within towns.

Non-Muslims are not admitted but the tourist can gain an impression of their incredible wealth by visiting less famous mausoleums where he is admitted: everywhere there are marble and precious metals; light pours down from crystal chandeliers and is reflected an infinitum on ceilings and walls covered by an intricate marquetry of small mirrors.

Other tombs, either more ancient (10th or 11th century) or commemorating persons of more local fame, often take the shape of a round or square brick tower — "gonbad (dome)" — decorated with attractive ceramic motifs, generally blue or black. The city of Maragheh is well-known as having several buildings of this kind. Sometimes the tower has a pyramid-shaped roof. The purest example of this architecture, and the largest (54m high) is the Gonbad-e Qabus, north of Gorgan. Mausoleums in honour of scientific, political or artistic personalities, unlike the major sanctuaries, have surprisingly sober outlines and decoration. Most of them are of recent construction, such as the tombs of Ibn-e Sina (Avicenna, the scientist) at Hamadan (1952), of the poet and mathematician Omar Khayyam at Naishabour (1934) and many others in all provinces. Most of these modern monuments are rocket-shaped towers.

Gardens, symbolic of refinement
There are only a few ancient royal palaces, "qasr". In Tehran, the Golestan Palace houses a museum; at Isfahan, Ali Qapu and the delightful Chehel Sotun (the Forty Columns) were for several years carefully tended by artists working on their architectural and decorative restoration (especially renovating precious frescoes). The charm of these and other palaces is enhanced by surrounding gardens which have often proved easier to preserve or reconstitute. Brick is a delicate material vulnerable to wind or to the slightest earthquake. This is why few large buildings date back to beyond the 19th century. Fortunately, the gardens — "baghs" — are of all ages. Those in Shiraz enable you, despite the presence of modern buildings, to recapture the much-described refinement of ancient princely courts.

A few high spots of the world of Antiquity
Persepolis alone is worth a visit to Iran. The breadth of vestiges of Antiquity, the noble beauty of ornamentations, the originality of some of the motifs, the imperial city's majestic mountain setting, the memory of the great historical events witnessed by these stones and so ably recalled in the "Sound and Light" show devised by Andre Castelot and Loris Tjeknavorian... all this contributes to an emotion which only the rare high spots of the world can provoke. But Persepolis does not reflect the whole of Iran's Antiquity. Archaeologists have unearthed extremely interesting vestiges, mainly in the west and the south-west of the country. In the Fars region, there is Pasargadae (Cyrus's Tomb and Palace), Naqsh-e Rostam (Achaemenian tombs, Sassanian bas-reliefs, fire altars), Bishapur (Shapur I's Palace and fire altars); in the Lorestan region: Shush (Susa), one of the world's oldest cities, and Chogha Zanbil, the finest "ziggurat" (staged tower) in the whole of the Middle East; in Kurdestan : the Taq-e Bostan caves, near Kermanshah, with sculptured walls, sculptured trophies in the Bisotun mountains, the Ganjnameh rupestral inscriptions, near Hamadan, formerly Ecbatana, dating back to the days of Xerxes. Several of these sites are deeply moving mainly because of the grandiose mountain or desert landscape, which surrounds them. The "ruins" themselves are fascinating for specialists. But they are frequently not evocative enough to be found really attractive by uninitiates.

Enamelled tiles, 13th cent., Iran Bastan Museum

Iranian arts

Prehistory, proto-history and ancient history are often a matter for specialists.

The layman admires the objects, inscriptions and jewels which have survived through the ages, he reacts to the elegance or strangeness of shapes and to the beauty of designs or of reliefs. He will have his full share of these in Iran. But he will need a qualified guide or a specialized book to interpret and understand the message transmitted by these testimonies of forgotten civilizations.

On the other hand, certain typically Iranian forms of art, still practised today, are to be found wherever the tourist goes. Certain architectural conceptions such as iwans, bare or enamelled brick decorations, the painting of miniatures or of frescoes based on these miniatures, poetry which all the people love, and carpets, the famous Persian carpets which as of the 17th century conquered the whole of Western Europe...

The following brief comments on these techniques and their development in modern times can help to make them better understood and therefore appreciated.

The "iwan" and the cupola, symbols of Shi'ite faith

"Mosque architecture derives directly from the spirit of the Koran", writes Seyyed Hosain Nasr, Dean of the Tehran Faculty of Arts and Letters, in the "UNESCO Courier". The external aspect of mosques symbolically reflects the various Divine Names and Qualities; the dome represents Divine Beauty ("jamal") and minarets Divine Majesty ("jalal"). History also has its role in sacred architecture. It is not by accident that the overall structure of Iranian mosques is different from that of sanctuaries to be found in the Maghreb, Egypt or Turkey for example. In the 16th century, Persia broke away from Sunnite Moslem orthodoxy and proclaimed the Shi'ite faith as a national religion.

As an affirmation of this religious nationalism, there was a generalization of the principles of construction which originated in the Khorasan region in the 13th century and were since applied to numerous provincial mosques, madrasahs and caravanserais. The Shi'ite mosque differed form the Abaasid mosques.

The most visible sign of this desire for originality is in the construction of "iwans".

Intelligent restoration

An iwan has the aspect of an apse open on the internal courtyard of the mosque or forming a porch with on each side, high vertical walls like those bordering a theatre stage. There are usually minarets at each end. The whole complex is covered with mosaics or bright–coloured ceramic tiles, and occasionally by mirrors arranged into geometrical compositions. The arch is sometimes covered with pendentives and stalactites forming a multitude of recesses and cavities the functional need for which is not always obvious. These astonishing constructions are sometimes very large: the southern iwan of the Imam Mosque in Isfahan for example, is 38 metres high and 26 metres deep. One often wonders how such a complex construction is shored up. If you obtained permission to go on the roof you would see a complicated system of feathered arches and buttresses which holds it up without being visible from the front side. (The same principle applied today made it possible to reconstruct the Abu Simbel temple, formerly carved out of a mountain).

Originally, iwans were nothing more than "mihrabs' oriented toward Mecca. Little by little this essential part of the sanctuary- it is from there that the imam directs prayers- was enlarged to become the main part of the edifice, overlooking the rectangular courtyard. The other sides of the courtyard were soon decorated with similar constructions, but usually smaller ones. *Cupolas* are not exclusive to Iran.

They are found in the whole of the Byzantine world, but Persian cupolas are exceptional by their size and by the richness, variety and colour of their inside and outside decorations. Visitors with some knowledge of architecture will notice how skillfully the passage from the hall's square plane to the cupola's circular plane is carried out, using an eight- or often sixteen-sided polygon. What cannot be observed, is that the cupola inside and the dome outside are not connected. They form two superimposed cups. In the empty space between them, there are buttresses and feathered arches which maintain the dome rigid while ensuring a certain flexibility as a protection against earthquakes. Some specialists observing Persian 11th –century mosques believe that this type of construction is at the origin of the Western Gothic arch.

The external dome is not, like the walls and cupolas, covered with mosaics or ceramic tiles, but with small, narrow bricks from five to six centimetres thick and of earthenware elements of the same thickness which make up a layer of protective masonry against rain, frost, wind … and pigeon's claws.

During the past few years considerable maintenance, restoration and consolidation work has been carried out on these magnificent buildings.

Mr. André Godard was for many years director-general of Iran's Archaeological Department and as such, was one of the initiators of this work. He writes that "cupolas have become once again splendid brilliant bubbles in the sky. They are really the world's most magnificent expression of enamelled architectural decoration".

The infinite variety of enamel decoration
The most ancient Islamic buildings were decorated with geometric motifs sometimes in relief, obtained by a skillful alternation of bricks placed obliquely edgewise, either overlapping or cut. This principle was maintained throughout the centuries and is still used for the decoration of modern buildings. The infinitely varied effects thus obtained are very striking. Binoculars or tele-lenses are frequently needed to observe them in full detail. Mausoleums, towers (mainly of the Mongol period at Qabus, Varamin, Maragheh, etc.), tall minarets (mainly in the Isfahan region) are decorated in this manner.

But as early as in the 12th century, polychromy appeared on facades and interior walls of religious buildings, first for practical reasons so that inscriptions (Koranic verses and dedications) could be read more easily, then for the purpose of honouring God by these embellishments. Mausoleums in Maragheh are among the rare buildings of that period still in good condition for which this technique was used. Turquoise, ultramarine and black are combined with the pink and red of natural brick.

Later there were the advocates of monuments decorated with coloured motifs and others who sought their effect in the proportions of the building, sometimes gigantic for the period. One approach did not exclude the other as can be seen at Soltaniyeh.

Polychrome decoration was achieved by a mosaic of pieces of handcut lustre faience, sometimes very small. This technique, still used in contemporary architecture, is called "kashi mo'araq" since the workers of Kashan- the "kashisaz" – are reputedly the most skillful.

The ornamental quality of calligraphy

At the beginning of the 17th century however, since Shah Abbas the First's ambitious building programme, the use of polychromy had become generalized, lustre mosaic was very often replaced by ceramic tile mosaic, less beautiful but much less expensive and much more rapidly applied.

The colours became diversified. Ochre- tinged yellows, greens, pinks and exceptional reds started appearing.

There was an infinite variety of motifs: geometrical compositions, flower elements, and in the 19th century, animals and human figures of Western inspiration.

But at all times *calligraphy* was the most popular decorative element both because of its symbolical nature and for its extraordinary ornamental value: Calligraphy of course is entirely based on the Koran, the Book of Books. Until recently the kind of painting which for centuries was current in Europe was unknown in Iran. Portraits or figuration of sacred personalities or events, although not forbidden, were frowned upon under Islamic religious law. Perspective, relief, light and shade were long unknown to Iranian painters.

Calligraphy, floral motifs and geometrical compositions were the sources of all decoration, while polychromy was restricted, as we saw earlier, to ceramics.

Finesse and subtlety of miniature art

Painting was entirely devoted to the illustration of texts: the Koran, scientific works, epic poems, imaginary tales, panegyrics lauding the achievement of kings and of real or legendary heroes. This was how the art of miniature started and developed. It is believed that the ancient source of this art is to be found in the predilection for painting demonstrated by Manikhaios, the religious reformer, the inventor of " Manichaeism" who lived in the 3rd century. Later, the illuminations in Byzantine manuscripts also influenced Iranian artists whose drawings got rid of the hieratism and stiffness of Christian models. Iranian miniature art is full of subtle delicacy. It is said that artists sometimes use a paint-brush with one single hair!

As early as the 11th century, the Iranians were the undisputed masters of miniature art and have remained so ever since. Today still, their skill is manifest, as can be seen by a visit to the Tehran Crafts School and its museum.

Persian artists excelled in this art largely because they avoided innovation from one generation to another. Pupils preferred to study in depth the lessons of their masters and to further refine traditional models. Evolution was slow. In the 13th century however, an appreciable transformation took place following the second Mongol invasion. Hulagu, a great patron of the painting art, encouraged the Herat and Tabriz schools. A Chinese influence appeared, mainly in landscape treatment : mountains, clouds, trees and running waters borrowed from Chinese painters took their place among bestiaries and natural histories. But this Oriental influence gradually wore off: Iranian originality once again dominated in skillfully composed and pathetic illustrations inspired by the national epic as described by Ferdowsi in his «Epic of Kings».

The end of the 15th century and the beginning of the 16th century were one of the peaks of miniature art. In Herat, forty calligraphers were permanently at work. At Tabriz, Behzad was directing hundreds of artists. A painter of

Persian Calligraphy 17th cent.

considerable genius, Behzad renewed the art by combining the traditional concept of decoration with a taste for realism and picturesque.

The compositions of this period underline daringly expressive attitudes, the wealth and subtle harmony of colours.

On large pages, scenes including a multitude of figures are arranged from bottom to top : distances are expressed by the superposition of objects; they are all equally lighted, leaving the scenery all its delicacy and the colours all their splendour.

Painting became frivolous and realist

Another evolution took place under Shah Abbas who was decidedly a reformer in all fields. Under the influence of painter Reza Abbasi, a certain degree of stark realism appeared in Iranian miniatures. He was the first artist who drew his inspiration directly from street and bazaar scenes in Isfahan. This was also the time when palace walls were covered with frescoes with warlike or frivolous themes (see Ali Qapu or Cehel Sotun) which were frequently reproduced subsequently. During the 19th century, miniature art fell slightly into disuse while Iranian painting opened up to Western influences. Mirza Baba, the official court painter, painted remarkably expressive portraits of princes (see two panels at the Azadi Tower in Tehran). He also painted chest lids, writing desks and the backs of mirrors in which one feels the influence of centuries of miniaturists' tradition.

This was also the period during which appeared in Iran naive mural painting called " coffee-house painting". Large frescoes or a succession of scenes whose style has been compared to that of comic strips served as a background for storytellers. They depicted the legendary heroes of Iran, "Rostam's battles", the adventures of Yusef and the ladies of Egypt", the " Bahram-e Gur hunts" with an approach similar to that of mediaeval Love Courts. This popular baroque

and naive art does not lack charm. The Iranian government made great efforts to preserve what is left of it. A large number of these paintings were brought together at the New Iranian Art Museum in Tehran for the greater joy of those who love spontaneous narrative art.

Contemporary Iranian painting is revealed to the international public in a Biennial which has been running in Tehran since 1958. Akbar Tajvidi, a painter from Tehran born in 1926, who is secretary-general of the Biennial, had this to say about it : "Iranian artists are increasingly trying to express themselves in a universal language which brings them closer to their foreign counterparts. This trend seems to result from changes which have occurred during the past few years at all levels of social life and which have also affected art"... Modern art was first almost completely rejected by the public, but soon artists and connoisseurs discovered in it a return to ornamental and bi-dimensional art, close to the Iranian tradition. " An original movement is taking shape, which differentiates Iranian modern art from that of other countries. It is noteworthy that Iranian artists have rarely drawn their inspiration from the world of machines; they are mainly attracted by decorative artistic expression. They are more deeply by surrealism than by expressionism...."

A very selective list of contemporary writers should include, among women writers, poet Simin Behbahani, from Tehran, and Mrs. Fourough Farokhzad who represented the "new" trend in poetry.

Among the men, the most original and may be the most talented poet is Fereidoun Tavallali from Shiraz who is known both for his knowledge of "ancient Persian" and for his modern poetry.

Other contemporary poets include Ahmad Shamlou, Mehdi Akhavan Sales, Nader Naderpur, Nosrat Rahmani....

Hejazi is among the good contemporary novelists

Persian Miniature 17th cent.

along with Afghani Ali Mohammad and Sadeq Choubak.

Sadeq Hedayat, now deceased, was a playwright who did several film transpositions. Rahi Mo'ayeri, who also died in 1970, wrote highly poetical songs, like those of Jacques Brel or Georges Brassens in Europe. Bastani Parizi and Dr. Shoja'-od Din Shafa are also worthy of mention.

The works of most of these writers have been translated into English.

Poetry, a source at which every Iranian drinks

In which country other that Iran would persons, men and women you meet during a journey there, and who are far from belonging to the literary circle intelligentsia, be able to quote the names of a dozen or so contemporary poets and ready to comment upon the works of two dozen classical writers?

In which other country a remote provincial city would name avenues and boulevards after writers whose fame dates back as far as six or eight centuries? Their statues enhance squares and monuments designed by the most famous modern architects mark their tombs. Even the daily press publishes poetry and devotes its columns to literary criticism and analysis.

Z. Safa, one of the best historians and French language translators of Persian literature (the other master in this field was Henri Massé) writes at the beginning of his "Anthologie de la poésie persane" (Gallimard 1964):

"Poetry is probably the richest and most brilliant expression of the Iranian genius. Born more than a thousand years ago, it has developed without interruption until our days (...).

"Every Iranian, even if he is not a poet, appreciates the beauty of verse; in a significant paradox, the most refined Persian poets are also the most popular ones (...).

"Whether epic, lyrical, didactic, amply narrative or, secret and intimate, light or serious, all styles of poetry reveal with remarkable consistency a specific kind of perception of the world which represents the spirit of a people. Linked with all phases of life, it is also the vehicle of philosophical meditation; it is through poetry that Iranians have expressed their deepest thoughts...."

A universal literature

Some names come up the most frequently in conversations, they are also those of authors whose writings are most frequently translated into European languages.

Rudaki, born in Samarqand and who died in 940, is considered as the "master of poets", the first Persian-language writer. He excelled in nearly all forms of literature, and wrote some fables which were the main inspiration for the famous French fabulist La Fountain.

Sa'di, from Shiraz, where he died in 1294, is considered as one of the richest and most subtle Persian language writers. His "ghazal" (short, somewhat lyrical poems) which celebrate profane love were throughout the centuries and still are very admired by Iranian women of all conditions.

Farrokhi, who preceded Sa'di by one century, is also considered as a master of romantic poetry.

Hafez, who is buried a few hundred yards from Sa'di, in the city of Shiraz they both loved so dearly and whose soft atmosphere pervades their writings. He died there in 1389. His works are maybe those best known throughout the world because of their innumerable translations. Z. Safa wonders whether he was: "A mystic or deeply attached to mundane pursuits which he celebrates maliciously in the style of the initiate? " " He was both", replies Safa, "like so many of his compatriots, because each of his poems and his verses contain such charm due to unsurpassable verbal harmony combined with so exuberant a flowering of images and meanings that it would

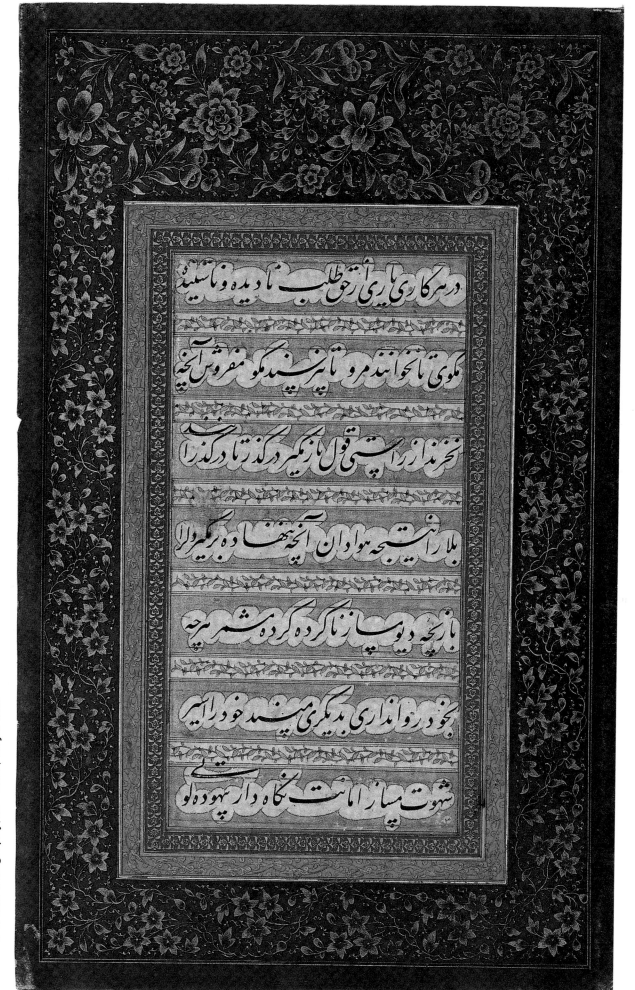

Persian Calligraphy, 19th cent., Qajar era.

28

Status of Omar Khayyam in Naishabour

Tomb of Sa'di in Shiraz

be a pretentious crime to make a definite choice…."

Omar Khayyam is also well known, at least by name, to Westerners. He lived and died in Naishabour in the Khorasan province where Persian literature was born in the 3rd century and blossomed in the 9th century. He was a scientist who challenged Islamic set ideas and certitudes, and had problems with the authorities. " His paradoxes and irony against dogmas and doctrine-pedlars, his blasphemy are due to revolt and not to scepticism. Khayyam's epicurism is never coarse. He exalts wine and love with soul-searing fervour. He extracts an imperishable perfume from his own sufferings". (Ali Now Ruz, " The Ruba'iyyat of Omar Khayyam", H. Piazza, 1923). His favourite form of poetry was the quatrain or "Ruba'i".

Sparked by religion and history
One of the reasons for the Iranians' passion for poetry is probably the very ancient origin of its tradition. *Zoroaster* himself, the reformer of Mazdaism during the 6th century B.C., wrote the first lyrics or "gathas" which are still taught today, assembled in the "Avesta": lauds in honour of Ahura Mazda, religious guidance, prayers, rules of conduct, comments on the prophet's conversations with " the Wise Lord". And history itself was expressed in poetry. The epic was always a source of inspiration. *Firdousi* (or Ferdowsi) was the absolute master of this form of poetry. In a sixty- thousand-verse poem, he relates the exploits of the kings and heroes who founded Iran. The "Epic of Kings" (Shahnameh) is an amazing sum of stories combining history and legend and in which generations spread out over a thousand years reap their share of heroism and imaginary prowess.

Everlasting Iran

Cyurs II, who reigned from 559 to 529 B.C., was not even the founder of the dynasty; it is one of his ancestors, King Hakhamanesh (Achaemenes) who is considered as the father of the "Achaemenians". He dominated the Aryan tribes settled since the 9th century B.C. in the Zagros and Parsumash regions then slightly to the south in the Parsa country. Other Aryan groups had settled even earlier in several regions of the high plateau mainly the Medes around Lake Urumiyeh (formerly Rezaiyeh) since 825 and Ecbatana (Hamadan) their capital in 722. Further back into history the Kassites (capital Babylon), the Elamites (capital Susa) were settled between Zagros and Mesopotamia. Beautiful objects and numerous inscriptions bear testimony to the value of these civilizations. Their evolution can be followed since the 4th millenary, that is to say six thousand years ago!

The Father of Human Rights
Ahura Mazda, "God of Light" was honoured throughout the country. In the middle of the 6th century, Zoroaster, a reformer of genius, codified, organized and purified the Mazdaism preached by the "Magi". Then why Cyrus? Because, during his thirty-year reign, he was the first to shape, buttress and organize the country; in the eyes of history he ranks with the great Pharaoes, founders of Empires who brought sudden progress to mankind . He was a unifier of divided peoples, a fair legislator concerned with the wellbeing of his subjects, a wise, just and tolerant conqueror. Even his adversaries, particularly the Greeks he fought bitterly, paid him these tributes. Here are the main chapters of his fabulous life (not including the golden legend which accompanies accounts of the birth and childhood of the future Emperor):

In 559, he succeeded Cambyses I, King of Parsumash and Parsa. By his mother, Mandana, he was also a descendant of the Median Emperors. In 550, he fought against Astyages, King of Media, and his maternal grandfather who had tried to eliminate him as a child. Media took sides with Cyrus, and he was proclaimed "King of Persia". He then undertook an astonishing series of conquests which reached its apotheosis when he made his triumphal entry to Tintyr (Babylon) in 538. He immediately showed the great political talent for which history was to honour him. He avoided destroying the sanctuaries of those he vanquished, he even offered sacrifices to their gods. He released the captives, including the Hebrews. He allowed them to return to Jerusalem and helped them to reconstruct the Temple. Barbarous customs related to the treatment of the vanquished were abolished. The famous Edict, considered as the first Declaration on Human Rights, has a Babylon dateline. Engraved on a small slightly ovoid clay cylinder, it has become one of the emblems of modern Iran. The original, unearthed at Babylon at the end of the last century, is now at the British Museum. The text is long, overloaded with dedications to the Gods: that is why only a few significant sentences are reproduced hereunder. The Empire covered Asia Minor as far as the Nile, and to the east, through India, stretched a hand out toward China. A new capital was founded in Pasargadae, in the Fars region and at the end of the reign a new city, larger and more luxurious, Persepolis, was built not far from Pasargadae. Governors, called "satraps", administered the provinces. Excellent roads and a system of messengers(foreshadowing modern postal services) insured rapid and reliable communications.

A human- headed capital from Persepolis, 5th cent. B.C.
◀ Iran Bastan Museum

It took about one week to send a message from Susa to Sardes (near Ephesus), the headquarters of the Asia Minor satraps. This means that the horsemen – messengers of the "Royal Highway" covered a daily average of 300 kilometres.

Darius, also the Great

Cyrus's son, Cambyses II, reigned for only eight years during which the Persians imposed their domination upon Egypt. He died without progeny. After some unrest, the Empire was firmly taken in hand by Darius, the first "Dariush" (army commander) who married Atossa, Cyrus's daughter, thus insuring the continuity of the Achaemenian dynasty.
Darius pursued and developed the achievements of his glorious father-in-law. His army became known as "immortal": its strength never fell below ten thousand men. Casualties were immediately replaced. The soldiers carried lances and a formidable bow with a longer range than any of those made at the time in other countries. After two years and nineteen battles, the new Emperor liquidated eight kinglets, pretenders to the throne which one sees bound and vanquished at the Emperor's feet in an expressive scene sculptured on the Bisotun cliff (between Kermanshah and Hamadan). Another army conquered western India. Navigators reac hed the Indian Ocean via the Indus River crossed the Persian Gulf and the Red Sea, up the present location of the Suez Canal. There, Darius got a canal dug between the Red Sea and the Nile river, thus creating a maritime link between the extreme east and the extreme east and the extreme west of the Achaemenian Empire.
Darius's major temptation, like that of Cyrus, was the conquest of opulent and luxurious Greece and of Athens the Arrogant. Greek colonies in Asia Minor had already fallen. The Phocaeans abandoned their city and thanks to a ruse managed to embark on an adventurous trip'

which took them first to Cyrnos (Corsica), then to Massilia (Marseilles). Cut off from Egyptian granaries, the Greeks also lost access to the forests (essential for ship-building) as a result of Darius's conquest of the Black Sea and lower Danube coast. All seemed ready for the Persian Emperor to add a glorious feather to his cap. Then came the Persian defeat at Marathon!

Persia- Greece: East-West

Persia had brought the West a thousand useful things: fruit, lucern without which there can be no cavalry, rice, pistachio, sesame, vines (may be), doves and peacocks. Persia taught it the meaning of the word "data" (law) , which is now used in several countries including in computer language.
Persepolis was completed and embellished in a thousand ways. The road system was expanded. The economy was prosperous, the currency healthy and trade exchanges fruitful. Documents show that salted fish from the Persian Gulf was being eaten in Anatolia and fish from the Nile was available in the Fars region. The sciences and arts flourished. All religions were freely practised. Greek scientists and philosophers made long visits to the formerly enemy Empire and were lavish in their praise of what they saw there. But the dream of a universal state was a persistent one.
Xerxes(486-465), son of Darius, had to cope with the Egyptian revolt at the beginning of his reign. This did not prevent him from becoming a prisoner of the Greek mirage. And Persia experienced another defeat, a maritime one this time at Salamis!
Like after the first defeat, the power and influence of the Persian Empire were hardly damaged. During the same year, 480, Xerxes further embellished Persepolis by building the Hall with Hundred Columns.
By an irony of fate, it was in this magnificent hall, symbolizing the wealth and glory of the

Median and Persian Guardians, Persepolis

Achaemenians that Alexander, banqueting there with his victorious generals, one hundred and fifty years later, himself initiated or simply underwent (the enigma is not yet solved) the great fire in the imperial palace. The magic "Sound and Light" of Andre Castelot's text and Tjeknavorian's music re-create this dramatic incident in the grandiose surroundings of the ruins of one of Antiquity's most beautiful cities. The Macedonian leader had also fallen for the mirage of a unified world. On reaching Persepolis, he may have thought for a moment that he had achieved his dream. His conquests had taken him from Egypt to India. Susa had yielded its immense imperial treasure. He thought he had achieved and expeditive amalgamation of the Greek and Persian peoples by ordering ten thousand soldiers from his army to marry local beauties while he set an example by marrying, in addition to Roxana, three Achaemenian princesses...

Alexander's ambition was to get the Persians to participate in the birth of a new, but still fundamentally Greek civilization. His policy was violently opposed by the army whose soldiers had but one desire: to return to Athens, Macedonia or Argolis.

The conqueror died (of fever or of poisoning?) at the age of thirty-three in Babylon.

Seleucids, Arsacids and Rome

His generals pounced upon the still rich remnants of Persia. One of them, Seleucos, reigned over the central part of the Empire. Hellenic influences remained in everyday life, arts and sciences (mainly in medicine). But it was not long before his successors were evinced. The "Seleucids" dynasty lasted less than a century. In 247, the Parthians who came from the east imposed their rule over Persia. Their chief, Arsax I, gave his name to the Arsacid dynasty. They reigned for nearly five centuries: from 250 B.C. to 224 A. D., that is to say during the

Roman civilization's main period of expansion. Their skill as horsemen enabled them on many occasions to vanquish Rome's heavy infantry. To the east, they waged an almost uninterrupted war against the Scythians.

At home, the Parthians gradually rejected Greek influences and ideas and adopted the Persian way of thinking. This evolution is reflected in works of art and coins (collections to be seen in Tehran museums).

In religious matters also, they returned to traditional beliefs and around the first century B.C., they restored Zoroastrism which was the religion of the Achaemenians who adored Ahura Mazda. The capital was settled at Ctesiphon, near Baghdad.

Among the Arsacid Kings: Tiridate, Ardavan, Farhad, Mehrdad, Orod... none were really distinguished, but during their reigns, Persia preserved its autonomy and recovered its personality.

The Sassanids: a great period

In the year 211 A.D. the Persians staged a revolt headed by a descendant of the Achaemenian dynasty: Ardeshir, who in 224 conquered Ctesiphon. A new dynasty started that of the Sassanids which was to reign for four centuries, until the Islamic Era. It was a prosperous period for Persia comparable in many ways with the Achaemenian period.

Zoroastrism was proclaimed as the official religion. The scattered texts of Mazdaism reformed 800 years previously by Zoroaster were assembled, studied and translated into the common language of the time, "Pahlavi" (or "Pehlevi" now known as "middle Persian ") .

They made up the "Avesta" the sacred poem, the collection of Persian holy scriptures. Fire altars were built all over the country (a few of them are still standing).

But as before, tolerance remained the golden rule of the Empire King Khosrow Parviz authorized

the Christians to practise their religion. Maniknaios (216-227) tried to achieve the synthesis between Christianism and Zoroastrism. He propagated the explosive ideas of "Manichaeism" which had repercussions in Spain with the Wisigoths and later with the Albigeois in France.

On several occasions under the Sassanid Kings, the Persian Empire almost regained the frontiers it had under Darius: the Mediterranean, the Nile and the Indus. But there was almost constant fighting against the Romans first, then against the Byzantine. Armenia remained a pawn for a long time. Rival armies swept back and forth frequently. In the year 260, the Persian Emperor Shapur I even captured Roman Emperor Valerian. The scene is illustrated on a bas-relief at Naqsh-e Rostam, near Persepolis.

These war-like episodes did not prevent the Sassanid Kings from being great builders. Palaces, dams, bridges, monuments and commemorative inscriptions are still visible in many parts of contemporary Iran. The Kasra Arch, at Ctesiphon (near Baghdad), the Shapur Palace near Bishapur (west of Shiraz) and the Taq-e Gara Palace are illustrations of the admirable architecture of the Sassanid period. Hunting scenes sculptured on the walls of the Taq-e Bostan Cave (near Kermanshah) are among the most eloquent testimonies of Khosrow II (end of the 6th century) both by their documentary value and by their artistic quality. Shapur I (241-272) is undoubtedly the most famous Sassanid King. A colossal statue, 8 metres high, in a cave near Bishapur, gives an impressive portrait of him. He was a great builder

and town planner. He founded several cities, including Gondi Shapur where he created a hospital and a medical school; it became later a famous university where during the 6th century scientists from India and Greece held congresses. In his "Epic of Kings", Ferdowsi writes at length

Sassanian Carvings, 6th cent., Naqsh-e Rostam, Fars

about Shapur I... "Guardian of the world, trustee of the treasures of the great and of the small"... Another sign of this happy period in Persia's history: King Khosrow Anoushiravan " the Great", whose reign lasted thirty- nine years in the middle of the 6th century, is still famous in Iran for his great sense of justice. He liked to act personally as a judge and was very good at it. He was also interested in science, and literature; under his reign numerous books were written or translated in Pahlavi language. He reportedly sent his vizier to India to fetch Bitpai's fables and the game of chess.

Unfortunately sovereigns of this kind tend to neglect the affairs of the state...

In such an atmosphere of refinement it was inevitable that watchfulness at the frontiers should relax and that the country become permeable to new ideas.

In neighbouring Arabia, Mohammad was preaching. Allah's horsemen were preparing to sweep from the Atlantic to China. Islam was at Persia's doors.

Islamized Persia, unshakably faithful to Ali

A name was at the origin of the religious and political revolution which was about to affect Persia: that of Salman-e Farsi (Salman the Persian). He was the first to establish contacts between Iran and Islam. He left the Fars region very early to join the real Prophet. Once in Arabia, he became one of Mohammad's most faithful companions, considered by the Prophet as a member of his family. Salman was also a close friend of Ali, the Prophet's own cousin and son-in-law. Salman was to exert a predominant influence upon the conscience of his Persian fellow-countrymen. He represented in their eyes a direct link with Mohammad's family and gradually converted them to the Shi'ite faith. This devotion to Ali's progeny also explains the important role played in Iran's "golden legend" of Ali's son Hosain and of all his family (in

Sheikh Lotfollah Mosque , 17th cent., Isfahan

680)... This theme was used upon innumerable occasions, by poets, painters and story-tellers. Political and military resistance was much sharper than in ideological matters. Proud of their Empire, the Persians turned out to be the Arabs' most determined opponents. The Arabs won a first battle against the Byzantines in Syria, then in 636, four years only after Mohammad's death, they vanquished the powerful Sassanid army at the battle of Al-Qadesiyyeh and seized their capital Ctesiphon. In 641, the Muslim armies won a second and decisive victory at Nahavand. Arab chroniclers described it as "the victory of victories" but it did not bring the war to an end since the King of Persia Yazdgerd III pursued the struggle with obstination until he was killed by one of his own subjects in 651. His son, Firuz, took refuge in China.

Deprived of its chief, Persia was conquered and incorporated into the Arab Empire. But its defeat was to transform itself into a special kind of victory: that of filling the cultural vacuum of the pious but rough and ready Arab society. Persian literature, philosophy, medicine and art were about to become a major element of Muslim civilization from Cordoba to Dehli, from Guinea to Samarqand.

In addition to this undisputed intellectual superiority, the result of a two thousand year old civilization, Persia also had the benefit of its craftsmen's mastery, the skill of its traders (who became the bankers of the new Islamic world) and of facilities it enjoyed because of its traditional position as a crossroads of the major "highways" of that period.

Thanks to this renewed importance and to their clear and distinct position on religious matters, the Persians were fairly rapidly able to regain their independence in their relations with the Arab invaders. It was a Persian, Abu Moslem, who, as the leader of troops from the Khorasan region, expelled the Omayids from Damascus and helped the Abbasid caliphs to conquer Baghdad. They frequently chose their ministers among Persians and Persian governors acquired a certain amount of local autonomy. In the year 822, the governor of Khorasan, Taher, proclaimed his independence and founded a new Persian dynasty. Others followed in a somewhat complicated pattern, but Persia was once again the master of its own destiny.

During the following century this revival of nationalism was to find its finest ferment in the " Shahnameh", the " Epic of Kings", by the poet Ferdowsi.

Turkish invasion absorbed

During the 11th century, the invaders came in from the north –east. The Turks gradually infiltrated the Khorasan region along the Caspian coast and arrived in Anatolia which became their new homeland. In the year 999, they were sufficiently powerful to dominate local Persian dynasties. Mahmoud Ghaznavi founded a vast empire. He even conquered northern India and helped to propagate in these remote lands the new Islamic – Persian civilization of which he was the principal protector.

The Seljuqs, his successors, asserted their domination from the Bosphorus to China. These sovereigns usually named Persians as ministers and Persia was a hotbed of intense cultural activity. Historians rightly consider the Seljuqs as an authentically Iranian dynasty.

"The Killer of people", " The Scourge of Allah", "The Anti-Christ" announced by a prophesy as arriving "from the land of Gog and Magog lying beyond the mountains of Asia, belonging to an impure and foul race, which does not drink wine nor salt its food, the cause of universal disaster"... These were some of the definitions chroniclers gave of Chengiz Khan.

At the beginning of the 13th century, a young chief asserted his authority over scattered tribes in immense Mongolia. An inspired organizer, a cunning and courageous fighter, he dreamt of creating an Empire of the Steppes, of federating all the world's nomads, of imposing the horseman's law upon city-dwellers imprisoned within their ramparts and their palaces and upon peasants, these renegades with mud on their feet. In all this he succeeded.

The Mongol plague twice wreaks havoc

In 1218, he came down from the Altai Mountains, marched through Transoxiana to Khorasan, occupied Persia, then turned east through India and China…. The Mongol chieftain reigned over the greatest empire ever created. Most of the countries he conquered never really recovered from the bloodshed and destruction he wrought upon them.

Holagu, one of the conqueror's grandsons, was left behind to reign over Persia. He very soon became "Persianized". Settled in Maragheh (south of Tabriz), he called Persian men of letters to his court and encouraged the sciences and arts. His progeny were converts to the Islamic faith; their dynasty was that of Ilkhan. Famous miniatures, obviously influenced by Chinese art and the magnificent "mihrab of Oljaitu" (who reigned from 1304 to 1316) were striking examples of the refinement of these Mongol sovereigns who rapidly forgot the steppes and their diabolical sortilege. But yet another conqueror, Turkey's Tamerlane (Teimur-e Lang), was to be seduced by the mirage of an Empire of the Orient.

In 1370, he entered into Iran. Over a period of thirty years, he conquered Iraq, Syria, Anatolia, Russia and India; he was about to invade China when he died in 1404. He chose Samarqand as his capital and his kingdom, while administered by Turks, was of Persian culture.

Tamerlane's disappearance was followed by a period of unrest. His descendants, the Timurids, were somewhat obscure sovereigns. It was not before the Safavid dynasty and Shah Abbas came to power in 1587 that Persia once again achieved a period of greatness.

Shah Abbas the Great

"Safavids" are named after Safi-od Din, master of a religious order whose leaders enjoyed considerable respect.

The founder of the dynasty, Shah Esma'il, was a descendant of a 13th century saint. He was supported by this powerful group of Turkish warriors called the Qezel-Bash (Red Bonnets) from Azerbaijan. Crowned King of Persia at Tabriz, his first action was to declare Shi'ism the "official" religion of Persia. The country was thus sheltered, both religiously and politically, from the domination of the Ottoman Turks. The capital was set up in Qazvin.

The Turks reacted by moving into Armenia and Mesopotamia and going as far as Tabriz. It was not before 1602 that Shah Abbas the Great succeeded in retaking that city; in 1623, he reconquered Baghdad. In the meantime, he vanquished the Portuguese settled at Hormoz on the Persian Gulf.

Shah Abbas, who reigned during the early seventeenth century, was a brilliant unifier, pacifier and administrator. But he was also a great builder. He created Isfahan! Under his reign, Persia started developing regular relations with Europe, encouraging foreign merchants to settle in the country (such as France's Chevalier Chardin who gave a vivid description of this period) and exchanging ambassadors with Spain, Great Britain and the Netherlands. (The Netherlands ambassador's gardener smuggled back a few tulip bulbs then completely unknown in Europe!)

After reigning for two centuries, the Safavids in turn were weakened. New invaders, the Afghans, crossed the frontier. They took Isfahan in 1722, and the Safavids' power started waning. The Turks felt it was time for revenge. And the Russians, whose power and territorial ambitions were on the upsurge, joined in the scramble.

Shah Abbas and the Emir of Turkestan, Chehel Sotun Palace, Isfahan

Nader Shah the Liberator

Persia found its saviour in the person of Nader, a mere non- commissioned officer of the Safavid army. He revealed his talents as an exceptional military leader. By a series of daring operations, he drove out the Afghans. In 1736, he was proclaimed Shah. The same year, he seized Uzbekistan and Iraq, thus restoring Persia's former frontiers. He also went into India and brought back among other things the famous Peacock Throne, which now enhances the splendour of the Golestan Palace in Tehran. After Nader Shah's death (1747), Afghanistan and Persia were soon separated and despite the close cultural, religious and historical uniting them, the two states maintained separate autonomy.

Zands at Shiraz, Qajars at Tehran

A new dynasty was created in Persia. The Zands claimed to be the followers and "regents of the Safavids". Their leader Karim Khan chose Shiraz as his capital. Fine mosques and bazaars were built there which are still to be admired. Meanwhile the Qajars, a Turkish tribe, had become very powerful. After Karim Khan's death, they took over the whole country, In 1779, Aqa Mohammad Khan conquered Tehran, which was only a small town, and made it his capital. During the whole of the 19th century, the city constantly grew and was embellished!

The Pahlavi era, a time for revival

Europe was becoming industrialized and the ensuing unrest inevitably had repercussions in the Orient. Still a feudal state, Iran became a battlefield for rival influences. The British and the Russians were the most aggressive. The former wanted control on the " Road to India" the latter were seeking an outlet to the Ocean through the Persian Gulf.
Naser-od Din Shah, who ruled over Persia for fifty years (1848-1896), took skillful advantage

Nader Shah Afshar, King of Afshar, 18th cent.

of the rivalries among European nations. The dawn of the 20th century witnessed an intensification of the "Great Powers" thirst for colonial hegemony. In 1907, the Russians and British signed a Persian trusteeship agreement. World War I did nothing to help Iran's affairs. The Parliament, created in 1906, was forcefully liquidated. The country was divided into two zones of influence, the Russian and the British. Like on so many occasions in the past, the situation was saved by an exceptionally strong and resourceful personality. In 1924, Reza Khan, an officer who had risen from the ranks of the army, unified the country, pacified the tribes, and initiated many administrative and social reforms. He acceded to the throne, adopted the name Reza Shah Pahlavi, and founded a new dynasty.

He was above all concerned by the creation of an economic infrastructure, by the building of roads, railways, factories (textiles and carpets) and power stations. He modernized the army and started a comprehensive administrative reform. Seeking to introduce European science and education, he founded the University of Tehran and modernized education at all levels. He decreed that the country would be called "Iran" since Persia was only one of its provinces (Fars). World War II prevented him from achieving other innovations. His son, Mohammad Reza Pahlavi, has taken over this arduous and glorious task.

He ruled Iran for over 38 years, until the victory of the Islamic Revolution on 10th February 1978.

A Zand prince, 18th cent.

Fath- Ali Shah, King of Qajar, 19th cent.

Ardebil Province

Name: also known as Ardabil.

Situation and access: Altitude 1,300 metres, 210 km N-W of Bandar-e Anzali, 70 km from Astara on a mediocre coast road then a twisting mountain track 260 km E of Tabriz via Ahar or 220 via Sarab.

It is surrounded by endless expanses of sheep-grazing ground without trees, snow-covered until April. Hamlets, which can hardly be called villages, try to shelter from the wind in hollows in the plateau. The houses are the same colour as the ground and there are more conic stacks of dung mixed with straw (the only fuel used there) than human dwellings.

When the snows start melting, people are seized by a kind of fever. Men and animals leave their shelters. The village-dwellers use sharp blades to speed the breaking up of drift-ice on the rivers. As soon as a few square yards of pebbles show up, sheep are put out to graze. On donkey or horseback, according to their condition, the peasants go to reconnoitre. Landowners use binoculars to supervise this tidying-up operation, a revival after a long period of hibernation. Bulldozers and lorries start work while camels, a strange sight, wallow in the mud and soft snow, superb and disdainful, carrying large loads of dry straw...

Sheikh Safi Mausoleum,
Neur Lake near Ardebil

41

A Khalkhali woman

East Azerbaijan Province
Tabriz

Situation and access: Provincial capital of Central Azerbaijan. Altitude 1,400 metres. 650 km N-W of Tehran. 310 km S-E of Bazargan (Iran-Turkey frontier) on a good road. 580 km N of Kermanshah by road including 100 km of track. Airport: Iran Air services. Railway: Istanbul-Tehran and Bakou-Jolfa-Tabriz lines.

Azerbaijan, one of these words which still sets off dreams. A whole colourful folklore comes to life.

Tambourine and sword dancers. Beautiful costumes. Women famous for their beauty. Hard-working peasants and willy merchants. A turbulent region, until recently torn by many invasions and military occupations. A country of sheep, therefore of wool for greatcoats, toques, blankets and skins worn by a whole population. A bitterly cold country during long winters, divided up by almost impenetrable mountain ranges which at the bottom of their valleys micro-climates enabling peasants to cultivate a few vineyards and fruit orchards. These are a few cliches the traveller brings along in his suitcase. They are valid but difficult to verify. There is only one itinerary which is really equipped and open during all seasons: the Bazargan - Maku - Tabriz - Zanjan - Tehran road, the traditional migration route. You need a lot of patience and a tough vehicle to reach these valleys.

Blue Mosque, National museum, Tabriz

43

Views of Tabriz
Tabriz Citadel (Ark).
Carpet bazaar, Maghbarat-ol Sho'ara
(Tombs of Poets), Kabud Mosque, The
municipality of Tabriz, the statue of Nazami, a
small tea house in bazaar, A tribal woman, a
Turkish musician (Ashiq), Ajil (Nuts of Tabriz)
the statue of Shahriyar (the great
contemporary poet)

45

In the bazaar, however, one seizes the originality of the town as a major agricultural centre. Armenians, Turkmans, Kurds work side by side in stalls piled ceiling-high with leather boots, woolen headgear, many-coloured fabrics and assorted tinmongery. Here again you will find the friendly bustle of the Oriental market with its mysterious discussions and its smell of leather and spices.

At the entrance of Tabriz, coming in from Tehran, a shady road leads to a large park with a wide expanse of water and a central pavilion. From this garden called "Il Goli", you can see a large red cliff overlooking the valley of the Taikel river which runs through Tabriz.

The village of Kandovan 19 km south of Osku in East Azerbaijan; its houses hewn out of volcanic caves, West Azerbaijan

West Azerbaijan Province
Urumiyeh

Name:Formerly (Rezaiyeh)

Situation and access: Province of West Azerbaijan. Altitude 1,340 m 25 km off the west shore of Lake Urumiyeh (landing stage at Golmankhaneh). By road 300 km from Tabriz, 280 km south of Bazargan (Turkish frontier, international post), 570 km north of Kermanshah.

"The most beautiful blue in the world" is how people used to describe that water, which contains a concentration of salt almost as heavy as that of the Dead Sea. The ancient Persians called it the "Royal Sea".

Apparently in olden times, when the water of the upper reaches of the lake were a good deal sweeter, the region had been even more fertile. There are traces of ancient civilizations all over the place. Nomad tribes frequented that "Riviera" as early as eight thousand years B.C. legend has it that Zoroaster was born there and we are assured that the three wise men from the east crossed the region on their way to Bethlehem. At Hasanlu, near Haidarabad (80 km S of Urumiyeh), around the southwestern corner of the lake, the remnants of tombs and rupestral homesteads have yielded glazed pottery as well as gold and silver objects.

Modern Urumiyeh is characterized by the joint activities and coexistence of Iranians of diverse racial groups and religions. People of Armenian, Kurdish, Turkish or Persian origin live side by side, as did once the Urartes, the Medes and the Assyrians. A Nestorian church with a tall, square belfry, dedicated to the Virgin Mary, has for its neighbour the Shi'ite Friday Mosque, its exquisitely sculptured mihrab is a splendid specimen of Seljuq art (12th & 13th centuries). A little farther down the road, a funereal tower — Borj-e Seh Gonbad — built in 1180, presents a geometrically ornamented facade in relief work, revealing the same influence.

Urumiyeh Lake, Maku City, Qara Kilisa (Church of Saint Thaddeus). West Azerbaijan.

49

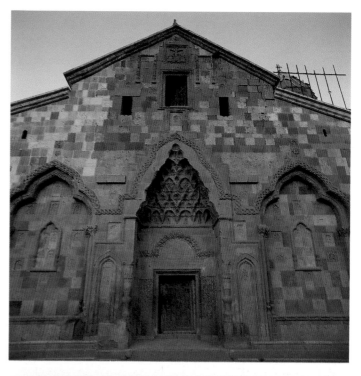

The Church of St. Stephanus, near Marand located 16 kilometers to the south-east of Julfa, dates back to the 8th century A.H. (14th cent. A.D.) and later, and is remarkable for its pyramidal roof cover and facade decorations. The monument is also known under the name of the church of Darreh Sham.

Khosrow Mirza Bath, 19 th cent., Maku

Urumiyeh bazaar

A Kurd woman of Maku

53

Bushehr Province

Situation and access: Provincial capital of Bushehr 320 km to the S-W of Shiraz and 1215km. S-W of Tehran.

The capital of Bushehr Province in southwestern Iran and located on the Persian Gulf, Bushehr is a major fishing and commercial port, and an export market for the farm produce of the neighboring and fertile Fars Province. Bushehr's industries include seafood-processing plants, and engineering firms.

The old section of central Bushehr has many examples of traditional Persian Gulf architecture from the period 1870 to 1920. The city was only a small fishing village before 1734 when Nader Shah chose it as the site for an Iranian naval base. At the end of the 18th century, the British and Dutch transferred their regional commercial offices to Bushehr , and during the 19th century the town was prominent as the home of the British political agent for the Persian Gulf. As a result Iranian resistance movement, Great Britain moved its diplomatic and commercial center across the Persian Gulf to the Arabian Peninsula at the beginning of the 20th century, an action that sent Bushehr into an economic decline. The city remained economically depressed until the 1960 s when the government initiated a major development program, including a petrochemical plant.

Because of are excessive heat in the Persian Gulf region, the siesta is taken very little except public transport functions between noon and late afternoon. Offices and shops close throughout the afternoon and reopen for a few hours at about 5 or 6 p.m.

Despite being largely desert, semi-desert or mountainous, limes and other citrus fruits, cotton, tobacco, and dates are grown in the region, There are more than 200 varieties of fish, among other marine life, in the Persian Gulf, but there are surprisingly little variety in the markets and restaurants, although excellent shrimps and prawns are widely available.

Views of Bushehr

Chahar Mahal and Bakhtiari Province
Shahr-e Kurd

Situation and access: Provincial capital of Chahar Mahal and Bakhtiari Province, 107 km to the S.W. of Isfahan 521 km to the S.W. of Tehran.

Bakhtiaris

The Bakhtiaris are the largest and most purely Iranian of all the Persian tribes. They belong to the Lor race and their language is closely related to the oldest known forms of Persian. The annual Bakhtiari migration in April from their Garmsir, or winter quarters in Khuzestan, to their Sardsir, or summer pastures in the Chahar Mahal region of the plateau south/west of Isfahan, takes from four to six weeks. It is an epic of human courage and endurance in which men, women and children of all ages, with their animals and household goods, travel by five different migration routes across some of the wildest and most difficult mountain countries in Persia in their search for grass.

The Bakhtiaris are divided into two major groups — the Haft Lang and the Chahar Lang —, which in turn are divided into tribes, sub-tribes and clans. No one seems to know precisely how many Bakhtiaris there are in Persia; one estimate, which may be on the high side, is of 450,000, perhaps half being migratory and pastoral, the rest agricultural and settled.

The Bakhtiari man and girl live permanently in the village of Karyak, about 120 miles south of Isfahan where the Kershan River, a tributary of the Karun, serves as the boundary between the Bakhtiari and Boyer Ahmadi tribes.

Chahar Mahal region

A Bakhtiari tent

Fars Province
Shiraz

Situation and access: Provincial capital of Fars. Altitude 1,600 metres. 500 km S of Isfahan (935 km from Tehran) on a good road. 300 km N-E of Bushehr on a good road in course of completion. 600 km E of Abadan on road in process of being restored. International airport and link-up with ran Air Internal airline.

An eight-kilometre-long motorway links the airport to the outskirts of the town, eight uninterrupted kilometres of rose-gardens, aptly announcing Shiraz, the "City of roses and poets".

Parks with magnificent trees are one of the town's attractions. Long wide shady avenues lead from one side of the city to the other. They are an incitement to leisurely wanderings during siesta time. Exemplary modern achievements, including remarkable hotels and very striking university buildings are conducive to a pleasant stay. Because of the city's altitude (1,600 metres) the climate is extremely pleasant; it is very mild in winter and not too hot in summer. Nearby Persepolis (now accessible by a main road) and the international fame of its annual art festival have confirmed Shiraz as a tourist centre. Several industries settled there recently including a very large petro-chemical complex. This gives the capital of the Fars region a new dimension, but does not prevent its inhabitants from demonstrating a touching devotion for their leading poets, Hafez and Sa'di...

' The populous quarters in the centre of the city are busy trading areas. The picturesque quality of the Iranian bazaar is enhanced here by the presence of nomads or semi-nomad elements belonging to southern Iranian tribes, including the Qashqais recognizable by the women's brightly coloured dresses.

Naranjestan-e Qavam (orange-garden), Persepolis bas-relief, a nomadic tent, all in Shiraz

57

Shiraz, Naranjestan, 19th century. This very beautiful house and garden which originally belonged to the Qavam family has now been restored to become the home of the Asia Institute. A fine painted tile frieze borders the roof, while the facade has a dado of carved stone slabs. The high central porch fronts a room lined with mirror mosaic, and the garden has been restored to an original design.

Next page, interior decorations of Naranjestan ▶

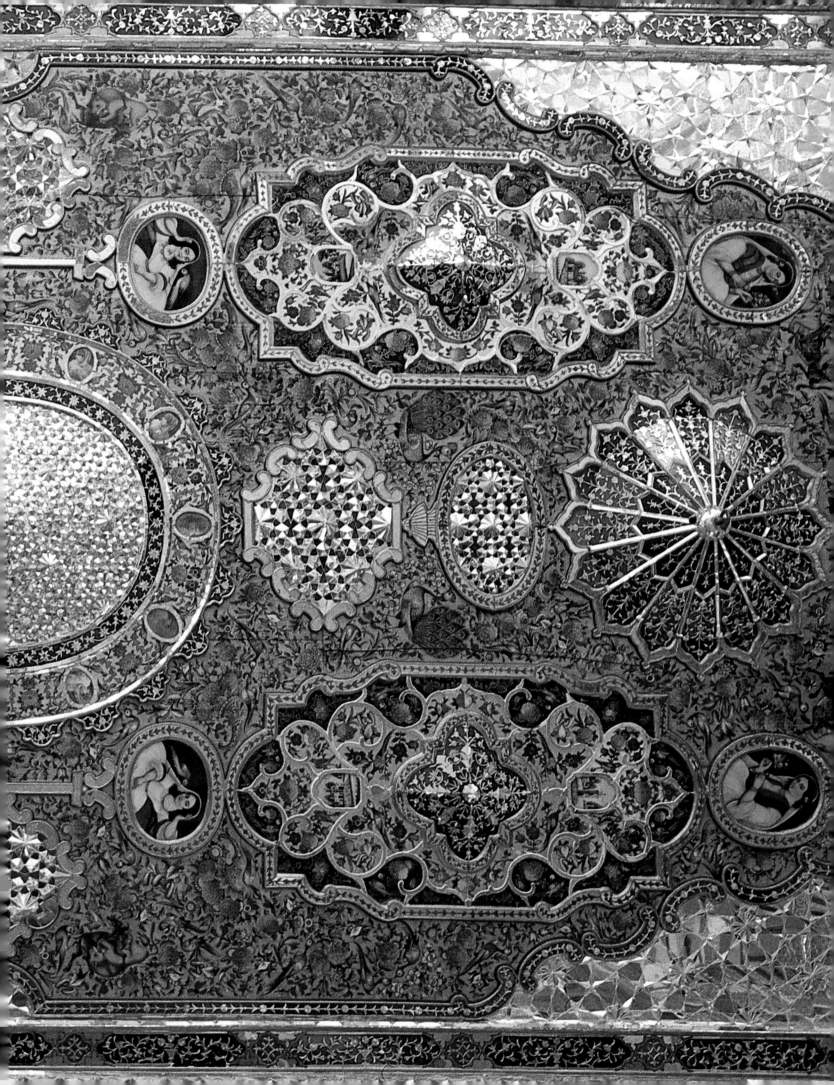

Sa'di died in 1291 at the age of 100. He asked for the following inscription on his tomb:

"From the tomb of Sa'di, son of Shiraz — the perfume of love escapes — thou shalt smell it still one thousand years after his death."

The many Iranians who come to visit these gardens of rest briefly place two fingers on the flag-stone of their favourite poet as a gesture of tribute.

Haft-tan (seven bodies) Mausoleum, 18th century.

The structure and tile decoration of the Nasir-al Molk Mosque, completed in 1888, closely resemble the eighteenth-century Vakil Mosque also in Shiraz. Its western prayer hall is enclosed on the courtyard side by stained-glass doors, and is used by the congregation during cold weather. Inside, two rows of six twisted stone columns with acanthus capitals support small tiled domes.

A Qashqai tribal chief, Mohammad Qoli Khan Ilkhani, built the idyllic Bagh-e Eram (Garden of Paradise) in the early eighteenth century, planting it with cypress, pine, orange and persimmon trees, and calling it after the garden of Paradise described symbolically in the Koran. About seventy-five years later, Nasir-al Molk bought the gardens, and constructed this elegant two-story pavilion designed by a famous Shirazi architect, Mohammad Hasan, who was also the architect for Nasir-al Molk's town house in Shiraz. The tiled rooms of the lower floor lie partly underground, and are cooled by a stream of water that flows from the house into a large central pool and down this rose-lined garden promenade.

Several other religious edifices are worthy of interest. The Old Friday Mosque has in the middle of its courtyard a building found in no other sanctuaries: the Khoda Khane - "House of God" - a square building (which reportedly imitates the Ka'beh in Mecca) and where the mosque's Korans are kept.

In the Fars Museum you shall find memories of Persian poets in the shape of beautiful calligraphies, technical masterpieces as well as illustrations of the grace and imagination of ancient writers. The museum is set up in a small octagonal pavilion in the centre of a charming garden. The rose is the dominant theme of all the decorations. In this page you can see portrait of Karim Khan Zand.

South of the river, the town stretches out, sliced into squares by large boulevards, Karim Khan Zand Boulevard forms the major axis. Most government departments and public services are in this part of the city.

An outstanding landmark is a portion of rampart, the remains of Karim Khan's enceinte, with an imposing bare brick tower, decorated with geometric motifs.

Hafez lived in Shiraz from 1300 to 1389. His verses are well-known to all Iranians and, six centuries later, have still value as aphorisms. His extraordinary popularity is due to his simple and frequently discursive language, rid of any affectation and to the use he makes of familiar images and of proverbial expressions. Iranians feel that his best poetry is the "Ghazal" (lyric) engraved on his tomb. The Ghazal (lyric) is a six to fifteen verse composition in which the verses are linked together by a unity of inspiration and of symbolism rather than by a logical sequence of ideas. Here are a few verses:

"Sit near my tomb, and bring wine and music — feeling thy presence, I shall come out of my sepulchre — rise, softly moving creature, and let me contemplate thy beauty.

The open space of a large esplanade to the south of the bazaar gives one a chance to appreciate from a sufficient distance the elegance or at least the originality of pear-shaped domes above a high tambour covering two mosque mausoleums: the Shah Cheragh and Seyyed Mir Mohammad Imamzadehs. The colour and geometry of the faience decoration is similar to that of a grass-snake's shrine. The facades of the two buildings are not shaped like those of traditional iwans. It is a portico supported by light columns in the style of houses in Shiraz. An interesting small museum has been set up inside the Shah Cheragh Mausoleum.

Shiraz, gateway to the south and rallying point for Iran's last nomads, offers in its bazaar an assortment of original craft objects. "Kilims" and "Jajims" are woven carpets and fairly light blankets with bright-coloured geometric designs. There are heavy silver bracelets and chest-plates with precious stone and enamel decorations. The delicate and patient work of Iranian craftsmen are to be found as boxes and marquetry objects.

The Qashqai nomads of Fars,. Number almost 150,000 people separated into five tribes, each divided into groups and subgroups. Their origin has not been clearly established, It is certain that they have been living in Fars for about three hundred years, but it is not known whether they came from the Caucasus or whether they are the descendants of the hordes of Genghis Khan and Tamerlane.

When no one any longer remembered whose tomb it was that stood alone on the Morghab plain, the Arabs invaded Iran, and impressed by the stone tomb of Cyrus the Great, called it the grave of Solomon's mother. In A.D. 1224, the Atabeg ruler of Fars had a *mihrab* or prayer niche carved inside the tomb chamber where the body of Cyrus once lay encased in a golden sarcophagus, and a mosque was constructed from the nearby ruins of Achaemenian palaces. Today the tomb of Cyrus again stands alone, the broad expanse of concrete and gravel may frighten away the nomadic tribes who used to pause on their yearly migrations to circumambulate the tomb, smearing mare's milk and honey on the steps; an offering to Cyrus, the mother of Solomon, or to the wind.

Shiraz, Naqsh-e Rostam. The gaunt beauty of the mountains, the immense landscape, the deep silence which pervades the site remote from any village, are appropriate for the sacred character of this necropolis sheltering the tombs of the main Achaemenian sovereigns (Cyrus lies in solitude at Pasargadae). From right to left, the tombs are those of Xerxes, Darius the Great , Artaxerxes I and Darius II. Darius the Great's Tomb is larger than the others.

Persepolis

Name:The site's Islamic name is Takht-e Jamshid, "The throne of Jamshid", a mythical King of Iran. The ancient name is "Parsa", "Pars's Town". Situation and access: Fars Province. Altitude 1,800 metres. 60 km N-E of Shiraz on an excellent road. 420 km S of Isfahan on a good road. International airport at Shiraz.National airport at Persepolis.

A large bare plain, surrounded by mauve cliffs with sharp edges. It is there, in the centre of the Marvdasht basin, that Cyrus the Great chose, toward the end of his reign, to build under the shelter of a fold in the mountains, a palace worthy of the empire. It was named Parsa, but later under subsequent Greek influences became known as Persepolis, "the city of the Persians".

You go to Pasargadae to contemplate, in the solitude of land deserted for the past two thousand years, the tomb of Cyrus, the founder of an empire. But you first go through Naqsh-e Rostam a sort of "Valley of Kings", dominated by tall ochre-coloured cliffs, cracked and wrinkled by the wind with half-way up, the cross-shaped cavities of the tombs cut right into the stone.

Without going into details the following excursion site are worthy of mention:

Bishapur (140 km to the W on the Ahvaz road), a large archaeological site in a gorgeous mountain setting, with the remnants of the palace of the Sassanid King Shapur (241-272 A.D.); the Qal'eh-ye Dokhtar Gorges, controlled by an impressive system of fortifications erected in the 10th and 11th centuries (near Firuzabad, 110 km S of Shiraz); other Sassanid fortresses near Fasa (170 km to the S-E); farther on the same road, in the direction of Darab (280 km of Shiraz) fortified enclosures, bas-reliefs and, at Darab proper, a queer, cross-shaped mosque hewn out of the rock.

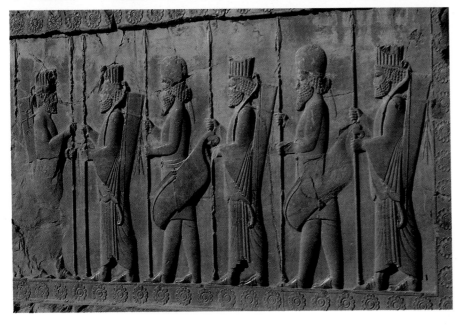

Achaemenian tomb and bas-reliefs, Persepolis, Fars

Persepolis, Fars Province. The many buildings which make up Persepolis are on an artificial terrace about 300 metres long and 450 metres wide, between 10 and 20 metres above ground-level. You reach the terrace by a monumental double staircase.

Sarvestan (Ancient Khwarestan) is about 80 km. from the main Shiraz highway, and is now a small town in the midst of orchards. There is little doubt about the age, only about the purpose, of the Sassanian buildings that lie south – east of Sarvestan. One can see from some distance the domes of the fifth century A.D. buildings, thought by many to be a hunting lodge or small palace built by Bahram V (A.D. 420 to 440).

Investiture of Bahram I by Ahura Mazda at Bishapur. The damaged area across the relief was caused by a water channel built against the cliff. The corpse below the king's horse was a later addition and may perhaps represent Bahram's grandson, deposed by Narseh.

Outside the town of Firuzabad, are the remains of Ardeshir Babakan's royal palace, one of the most beautiful of Sassanian edifices. The palace consists of several iwans with crescent vaultings, a number of rooms with domical roofs, and a courtyard. It is a rectangular building, 140 meters long and 55 meters wide.

Bishapur is the original name of the town of Shapur 25 kms west of Kazerun, where there are ample remains from the Sassanian period. These remains are incontestable proof of the town's prosperity and splendor during the reign of its founder, Shapur I, and throughout the Sassanian era.

Among the important historical monuments of Bishapur and Tang-e Chogan, first and foremost is a huge statue of Shapur I installed in a grotto on top of a mountain, by the King's order. This stone statue is some seven meters high and lay on the ground for many years, broken in parts and covered with thick layers of dust, until it was restored in 1957, and installed on a strong pedestal in its present erect position.

Gilan Province
Bandar-e Anzali

Situation and access: Region of Gilan. Large port on the Caspian Sea. Altitude - 20 metres 380 km N-W of Tehran via Qazvin and Rasht, on a very good road or 430 km via Chalus on a good twisting road.

You drive your car across the beach, which shows that the sand there is hard and pure.

In a pleasant and relaxed atmosphere its inhabitants and seamen or shore-goings stroll during the evenings and the whole Friday in the public garden which follows the coast road on the right bank of the channel linking Anzali Lake to the sea. When you become tired of walking, you sit down on a small wooden stool, have a cup of burning-hot tea (chai) and nibble pounds of pistachios while watching the boatmen wielding with calculated slowness the oars of their gaily coloured craft.

World capital of precious caviar

Bandar-e Anzali is the capital of caviar. The preparation and marketing of the precious black eggs is a state monopoly, handled through "The Iranian Fishing Company" coming under the Finance Ministry. The public is not admitted to the immense refrigerated hangars (-18 degrees centigrade) where tons of sturgeons, monsters between 2 and 3 metres long weighing between 75 and 100 kilograms (the record is an 850-kg animal) are stored after removal of caviar usually equivalent to about one tenth of their weight. Nor is it easy to approach the fishing boats or equipment.

Bandar-e Anzali, Gilan Province, daily life

Views of Bandar-e Anzali

On the way to Asalem, Gilan Province

As one descends from the plateau toward the Caspian Sea, one will discover forests, wooden houses and granaries mounted on wooden pillars.

Forest dwellers , Talesh, Gilan.

Women carrying tea leaves, coming back from their work, Fuman, Gilan

Tea fields and Qasemabadi traditional costume, north of Iran

Masouleh

A two-hour drive from Rasht across rough roads brings you to the village of Masouleh where the architecture intimately relates to the rocky mountain terrain of Gilan. Houses hug the cliffs, rising vertically upward, with rooftops and village streets virtually indistinguishable.

Cattle herding is the main village occupation and delicious white cheese is sold in the small tea houses lining the streets.

Masouleh Village, Gilan, north of Iran

Gilan Province, rural houses

90

Masouleh Village, a traditional shoemaking, Gilan Province

Places like this village of Masouleh hidden in the green vegetation of the Caspian region or like Bam, the historic city bordering on the Great Desert partially fertilized by irrigation, illustrate the rich variety of contrasts found in this immense country.

Siyahkal nature, Gilan, north of Iran

Dailaman nature, Gilan, north of Iran

Gilan Province, a landscape of the wild nature of Talesh region

For the foreign visitor, the hinterland, even more than the beach, constitutes an astonishing discovery.

Upstream from the Lushan Dam the landscape changes.

The vegetation, crops, houses and people are suddenly different from what one sees on the Iranian plateau.

The countryside is covered with greenery. Real trees surround houses no longer made of brick, but of wood with thatched roofs. There are hundreds of these small houses with balconies, flanked by barns or granges on pile columns and scattered on the slopes of the valleys or on hillocks on the plain.

Astara (140 km from Bandar-e Anzali) was the scene of renewed activity in 1975 since trade exchanges with previous Soviet Union resumed in order to relieve the overloaded trading post of Jolfa (N of Tabriz).

Hundreds of lengths of piping stored at the entrance of the village recall that here the natural gas pipeline from remote Abadan enters Soviet Union previous territory.

98

The wedding ceremonies of forest dwellers, Talesh, Gilan Province

Shanderman, Thursday Bazaar, Gilan

Taka ceremony, spring's harbinger, forest dwellers, Talesh, Gilan

Golestan Province
Gorgan

Situation and access: Altitude 20 metres. 381 km N-E of Tehran on a good road via Mazandaran. 131 km W of Mazandaran, on a good road. 564 km W of Khorasan on a good road.

To the west of Khorasan is the newly-founded province of Golestan. This was formerly a part of Mazandaran province, and enjoys the temperate weather of the Caspian region. The region has a large number of Turkmen inhabitants, many earning a living by weaving their characteristic rugs. Near the provincial capital Gorgan, a conical 10th century tower is famous as the mausoleum of the local ruler, Qabus Ibn-e Voshmgir. The province has large tracts of protected forests.

The Turkmen of the Gorgan steppe are one of the non-Persian peoples inhabiting Persia, first arriving there in the 11th century during the great Oghuz migration from Central Asia. The Atrak River separates them from their brother Turkmen in the republic of Turkmenistan.

Loveh waterfall, Aq Qala bazaar, Golestan Province

Mazandaran Province, Aq-Qal'eh, or White Fort, in Turki, is a small market town in the heart of the Turkman steppe, 12 miles north of Gorgan. Early each Thursday morning Yamut Turkmans from the surrounding countryside assemble there for the weekly market, a special feature being the horses and tribal rugs brought for sale.

Qabus Tomb, rug sellers, Aq Qala bazaar, Golestan Province

Golestan Province, Bandar-e Turkman. The Turkmans make much use of felt, particularly as roofing and floor covering for their tents, and as saddle cloths for their horses. The rolling process illustrated here lasts several hours and is designed to compact and straighten out the newly made felt so that it will lie flat.

Golestan Province, Turkman dwellings at Bandar-e Turkman. These circular tents with walls of matted reeds and roofs of felt and horsehair, are similar to those of the Turki-speaking Shahsavan tribes of north-western Persia, but quite unlike the rectangular, black goat hair tents of the Bakhtiari, Qashqai, and other nomadic or seminomadic tribes of the country.

Hamadan Province

Name: Ancient name Ecbatana, also Hamedan
Situation and access: Altitude 1,800 metres. 400 km
S-W of Tehran on a good road, via Qazvin. 190 km
E of Kermanshah on a good road. 530 km N-W of
Isfahan on a good road with short stone-scattered
passages, via Aligudarz. 330 km W of Qom, via
Arak, on a good road with one stone-scattered
passage.

A large central roundabout with six avenues running into it: this is what a simplified plan of modern Hamedan looks like. Nothing is left of ancient Ecbatana, the Medes' capital before they formed a union with the Persians. Ferdowsi the poet, says it was founded by Jamshid, a king who was maybe somewhat hastily described as legendary. (Admittedly, Homer's works tend to be used as a travel guide for modern Greece). There are not even a few old stones in any museum, and there is not much to be said for a misshaped "lion" similar to those which decorated the tombs of Parthian officers. A more interesting sight for tourists who may not have seen any before, are the cuneiform rupestral inscriptions engraved on a cliff at the bottom of a green valley about 10 kilometres west of the city, the site is called Ganjnameh.

While lacking antique vestiges, Hamedan, has several monuments worthy of interest. They are usually mausoleums. Their exterior was recently renewed by constructions inspired by the spindle - shaped structure of Mongol towers, to the exclusion of all other features of these towers. The best one covers the tomb of the famous Ibn-e Sina called Abu Ali by the Persians and Avicenna by the Western world.

Another poet honoured in Hamedan, is Baba Taher, who lived during the same period as Ibn-e Sina.

Hamedan's most curious monument is a Jewish mausoleum reputed to contain the tombs of Esther and Mordecai. Esther was a young Jewish girl who came to ask Xerxes for just treatment and protection for the people of Moses.

Tomb of Avicenna, Lalejin pottery, Hamedan

Ganjnameh, Achaemenian inscription

Baba Taher Tomb

Hormozgan Province
Bander Abbas

Name: perpetuating the memory of Shah Abbas the Great who founded the town after his naval victory over the Portuguese off Hormoz. Previously called Gameron or Qamerun.

Situation and access: Altitude: sea level. Port in the middle of the strait linking the Persian Gulf to the Sea of Oman. 500 km to the south of Kerman by excellent road. Airport; regular flights by Iran Air. Railroad projected.

A combination of social, commercial, military, political imperatives — and tourism — have turned Bandar Abbas into one of those Iranian towns where the desire of the central government to modernize and develop even the most outlying provinces as keenly as the big urban centers is the most manifestly spectacular.

Controlling the strait of Hormoz, one of the world's neuralgic areas, Bandar Abbas occupies a strategic position of the greatest importance. In the 16th century already (in 1520 to be precise) the Portuguese, intent upon protecting their Indian empire, took possession of the Isle of Hormoz. They were expelled in 1622, after a tough naval battle, by Shah Abbas the Great who founded the town which has been bearing his name ever since. At the present time, when the world's mightiest tankers sail past its waterfront almost in bucket-chain fashion, Bandar Abbas represents a trump card for world peace.

Close to the Arab world and, through the Sea of Oman, open to the oceans of Asia, Bandar Abbas is the natural maritime outlet for Iran. On the beach of the village of Tiab, some 100 km farther east, porcelain shards of great antiquity may be found, showing that the Chinese had once known this sea-route. Its significance today is enhanced by the modern docks which have been excavated there; cargoes of all nationalities call at the port to unload cement and cereals, motor vehicles and machinery.

A few hundred yards out at sea scores of fishing barges and small Arab sailing boats, with tall prows and forecastles reminiscent of another age, seem to be looking on indifferently. Their sombre silhouettes resemble the outlines of a fortress on the Qeshm Island after which they have been named. A considerable part of the local population lives on the proceeds of its fishing activities. They still employ the traditional net, but soon modern methods of preservation and transport will permit Iranian coastal fishing to be extended and brought up-to date. The drying sheds worked by wood smoke which the Danes installed a long time ago are now shown in the curing plants as mere museum pieces. Meanwhile the animal life of those warm seas, not yet overly polluted despite the presence of oil-tankers, is being studied in specialized laboratories.The great damp heat does not start before May and becomes unbearable only between June and September.The beaches are covered with silky sand, cleansed by fairly ample tides. Their gentle slope provides a safe playground for children.

Young sailor, traditional Mask, Bandar Abbas, Hormozgan

Here, the urge for rapid new achievements obviously proceeds hand in hand with a concern to embellish the rather austere natural environment. All sorts of trees are being planted, and notably a shrub, the "ghar zanghi", which grows by tiers, pushing out horizontal branches at a higher level each succeeding year. The gardens abound with flowers, grown and maintained at the cost of copious watering. The bigger buildings are mostly constructed in keeping with local architectural tradition - honeycomb-cum-cupola arrangements will shelter television sets, for example, or ancient cisterns covered by a large dome be turned into a nightclub or local museum.

Antique monuments are restricted to a disaffected Hindu temple with its characteristics, conical roof, a Shi'ite mosque, bare of any particular kind of ornamentation, and, as a symbol of the closeness of Arab influence, a Sunnite mosque complete with a slender, cylindrical minaret, supporting a wooden balcony.

Nearby is the bazaar with its covered streets reserved for small retail trade. Hardly anything picturesque would be found in those tiny shops — sometimes not bigger than a cupboard — were it not for the queer variety of manufactured goods smuggled to Iran from the four corners of the world. That practice has been tolerated from times immemorial, for the customs are operative only at the provincial frontiers. The articles sold bear the mark of, our time. Television and transistor radio sets are displayed by the hundred, yet sometimes this bazaar trade can also present charming anachronisms. Such as the vendor of electronic calculating machines who counts his earnings every evening with an abacus...

Bandar-e Pol (Port), Kharbast cave and Galehdari Mosque, Hormozgan, south of Iran

Hormoz and Qeshm, splendid holiday resorts

The two islands are clearly visible on the horizon from the beach at Bandar Abbas - Hormoz on the left, and Qeshm on the right. They can be reached in two hours by motor-launch.

Qeshm is very large (almost 100 km long); few tourists can pretend to know it.

Hormoz appears to be bristling with pointed mountain peaks. The island is round with a beak jutting towards the mainland. The headland is occupied by a large village, a fishing port, a magnificent beach and, on a rocky promontory, a fort. Its walls and towers, although damaged, are still impressive. The strange thing about this edifice is its colour - an intense red veering to purplish-blue. On taking a closer look at its walls they reveal themselves as being built of coral blocks. In the middle of the fort two large vaulted cisterns bear witness to the size of the building. It is what remains of the Albuquerque stronghold built in 1520. Hormoz (or Ormuz) had been a prosperous town at that time, an early link between East and West. Its conquest by the Portuguese was no easy matter. It was said that the admiral in command had made a vow not to trim his beard until such time as he entered the town. Once that happened the invaders remained there for a century and two years.

Today, the hovercraft of the Iranian Navy land regularly on the beach, the ochre-coloured sand of which is gradually burying the citadel.

In the near future peaceful battalions of holidaymakers will, in turn, invade Hormoz, the colourful island. It peaks are ready for the mountain-climbers, it creeks for the skin-divers, its ancient stones for the amateur archaeologists and it beaches for those wise people for whom a bit of sun, tranquillity and crystal-clear water suffice to forget the turmoils of this world.

Indian temple, fishing vessels, water-cistern and a view of Kish Island

Laft wind-towers, south of Iran

The road to Kerman, of remarkable design, climbs gradually, crossing several parallel barren mountain ranges.

Having passed through the large town of Sirjan (310 km from Bandar Abbas) the road hits a mountain pass at the altitude of 2,500 m flanked by a peak 4,375 m high. Between these grim mountain ranges there stretch fawn-coloured plains where herds of gazelles are revealed by whirling clouds of dust rising in their wake.

At first, about 50 km after leaving Bandar Abbas, a narrow road branching off on the left towards Fin leads to a narrow ravine from which rises a boiling source of green water discharging sulphur fumes. This source of Qenon is supposed to be good for healing skin diseases.

Only a few kilometres further on, the main road crosses a curious bit of scenery a narrow valley, the steep rocky sides and the bottom of which, the latter bordering a stream, are white as if covered by snow. It is in fact crude native sodium carbonate, glistening under the sun.

Branching off the Kerman road an asphalted trail turns east, some 10 km from Bandar Abbas, in the direction of Rudan and Minab (about 120 km).

The road leads through savanna-type country interspersed with numerous trees with thorny branches and gnarled trunks. In fact, except for the region bordering on the Caspian Sea, few parts of Iran boast such a dense vegetation. Panthers are said to be haunting the countryside where patches of cultivated land alternate with soil left fallow. Near Minab, date-palms begin to show up. The town participates in the economic development of the entire region. The bazaar is a replica of the one in Bandar Abbas.

Lanj (fishing vessel) building in Kong, port children, Kong Mosque, south of Iran

Isfahan Province

Name: also called Esfahan, Isfahan. Situation and access: Altitude 1,430 metres. 490 km S of Tehran on a good road via Saveh; 435 km via Qom (155 km); Tehran - Qom motorway under construction; 500 km n of Shiraz on good road; 530 km S-E of Hamedan on good road with stone - scattered stretches. International airport.

Planned railway liaison through link with line serving Riz.

..."The city of Isfahan, including its outskirts, is one of the largest towns in the world... The Persians say, to describe its size: "Isfahan nesfe Jahan, i.e.: Isfahan is half of the world."

"What is admirable in so large a city with so many inhabitants is the abundance and opulence which reigns despite the absence of sea or of a navigable river. What seems unbelievable is that the city obtains most of its food, except livestock, from an area of not more than ten leagues around it. The area contains no less than fifteen hundred villages; one must admit that most of its surroundings are incomparably beautiful and fertile..."

An exceptionally mild climate

"The climate there is healthier than in any other part of the world. A proverb says: "Who comes to Isfahan cannot fall ill, who comes there ill will see his health restored". This is because of the air, which is extremely dry and subtle. There is extreme heat and cold, but the cold does not last more than three months. It snows in winter but rarely. Rain usually falls in March and April, probably because of vapour from melting snow. A west wind blows gently throughout the summer, it starts when the sun sets and it is so cold at night that you often need to wear a fur-lined coat. Spring starts in February, the weather becomes balmy and admirably beautiful. At the end of the month, gardens are covered with flowers and the trees are blooming, especially the almond trees".

Jame' Mosque, engraved handicrafts, passageway of Sheikh Lotfollah Mosque

113

There is little to be changed today in these travel notes by knight Jean Chardin on Isfahan -as we usually write now- where he lived between 1673 and 1677, three centuries ago. The term "admirably beautiful" to describe the city which was the capital of Persia is roughly the one used by hundreds of thousands of tourists attracted by the flower-decked domes and the giant minarets with their enamel corsets and wooden collars.

Photography made the silhouettes of these buildings familiar, but it has neither detracted from their mystery nor dampened the emotion provoked by their discovery.

The monuments of Isfahan rank among the very rare works of which one can say that the more you behold them the more they surprise and fascinate you. This is why a visit to Isfahan is never complete. After seeing all the listed marvels, you go back to the river or to the Imam Square, to the oasis or the ancient districts.

Admirably beautiful and unblemished

This royal city which was the standard-bearer of Muslim Persia's Great Century is full of reminiscences; some are engraved on the walls of the palaces but the tourist hardly notices them, fascinated as he is by the unreal blue colour of an ornament, by the elegance of a column hewn out of cedar wood, by a thin ray of light filtering through a hole in the keystone and shining upon the inner facing of an enormous cupola decorated with stars and arabesques.

An excellent initiative. But one must admit that most visitors, dazed by so much beauty, hardly pay any attention to these explanations. Some, subjugated, do not dare penetrate into the courtyard, a strange closed world, others keep moving from one corner to another, attracted by incredibly intricate details in wall decorations, then by the dark entrance to an iwan, or the sunlit pool in which the tip of a minaret reflects. Beauty assumes a new dimension.

Chahar Bagh Ave., Vank Church

The Zayandeh-rud river runs through the town from the west eastwards. It is crossed by five bridges. A canal bridge is not open to traffic.

A town where you cannot get lost

Each bridge coincides with a straight avenue running through the city from north to south. The most important one runs through the centre of the town. It is called Chahar Bagh which means "four gardens", the four sectors of this garden city are marked by the cross made up by the river and the main avenue which leads to the Tehran road to the north and to the Shiraz road to the south; the bridge used by this large highway is the famous "Thirty-three Arch Bridge "(See-o Seh Pol" or "See-o Seh Cheshmeh"; pol: bridge) open to motor traffic only in the north-south direction.

A few hundred metres upstream, i.e. west of Chahar Bagh, a modern bridge carries traffic in the other direction.

The town's westernmost bridge (Pol-e Marnan) is not open to traffic; it joins two avenues, which form a kind of circular road. This is a district of mechanics, coach workers and car-repair shops.

In the eastern part of the city, Hatef, Neshat, Chahar Bagh-e Sadr Avenues form a long artery leading from the north-eastern popular district to the Khwaju Dam-bridge and beyond that, to the airport. The town constructed by Shah Abbas and the Safavid Kings lies between these avenues and Chahar Bagh Avenue.

Meidan-e Imam (formerly the Royal Square) marks its approximate centre with, to its south, the mosques and palaces, to its north, the labyrinth of the bazaar, and a constellation of mosques, mausoleums and madrasahs in small streets. The Friday Mosque (Jom'e Mosque) is in the northeastern part of the old city, on Hatef Avenue.

Atashgah (Sassanian fire temple), Gar Minaret, Dar-ol Ziafeh Mosque

There are two landmarks which visitors can identify easily alongside the central portion of Chahar Bagh Avenue. First, the dome and two minarets of the Madrasah formerly Chahar Bagh (the School of the Shah's Mother or Sultani school) next to the famous Abbasi Hotel with its bevy of tourists, buses and taxis. The second landmark is the white City Hall building at the intersection of Chahar Bagh Avenue and Sepah Avenue leading to the Meidan-e Imam. Almost opposite the "Madrasah Chahar Bagh", a long succession of avenues: Sheikh Bahaei, Saremiyeh, etc. leading to the Shaking Minarets Mosque and to the western side of the oasis.

The districts to the south of the river (right bank) are developing rapidly. Buildings include government departments such as the television service, new factories and almost at the foot of the mountain, a large university. Near the river and to the right of Chahar Bagh Avenue lies Jolfa, the Armenian quarter with its cathedral and small churches. Nazar Avenue leads there.

Among all the cities of Iran, Isfahan is the one where it is the easiest for foreign visitors to find their way thanks to lighted panels at crossroads indicating the name of the main highways.

Jolfa: Christ in Shah Abbas' Kingdom

There are still about eight thousand persons of Armenian origin who freely practise the Christian faith in the heart of Muslim Iran.

There are thirteen parishes. The first church to be built in the new Jolfa was tiny St Jacob which is now on the grounds of St Mary. Along with Bethlehem, St George "(or Qarib)" and St Saviour Cathedral (called "Vank", the Great), St Mary is the most interesting church to visit. These sanctuaries are very richly decorated. Latin, Russian and Persian influences mingle in an intriguing manner. Tapestries, mosaics and paintings are done with oriental techniques, but the subjects illustrate, with an approach familiar to Westerners, the episodes of the Bible and of the Evangil.

Khwaju Bridge, Baba Rokn-od Din and Shahshahan Mausoleum

Turning back toward the city, the first bridge encountered is the Khwaju Bridge (named after a neighbouring district). It is a magnificent structure with two tiers of arches. The lower arches are fitted with locks. When they are lowered, a small lake forms opposite the royal palaces built under Shah Abbas II (1650) on the right bank. In the middle of the bridge, the King got a pavilion built, which is still intact. On each of the bridge's piers, he got stone seats built so that his subjects could sit there to watch the Zayandeh-rud river.

Another extraordinary bridge is the See-o Seh Cheshmeh (thirty-three arches), also called Allahverdi Khan Pol (Allahverdi Khan Bridge), after the architect who built it in 1600 and who was also Abbas the Great's army chief. The bridge is about 300 metres in length. A row of delicate arcades (about 100 of them) lightens its silhouette and lengthens its lines.

One really can not call "river" a trickle of water which disappears in the sands! But the trickle of water takes its source in the Zagros mountain range 400 kilometres away. Although it is not navigable, it brings life to dozens of oases, as well as coolness and greenery to Isfahan itself Dams store up part of its waters for the "Mobarakeh" steel complex.

The Friday Mosque, the most ancient one

There are two hundred mosques in Isfahan. Visits to three of them are therefore not superfluous all the more so since Imam, Sheikh Lotfollah and Friday Mosques differ considerably.

The Friday Mosque (Masjed-e Jom'eh) is the oldest. The greater part of the present building dates back to the 11th century and to the beginning of the 12th. Changes and additions were made in subsequent periods. The monument therefore illustrates the evolution of Iranian sacred architecture. Comprehensive restoration and clearing work around the building have been carried out during the past few years. The central courtyard is one of the largest in Iran: 65 by 76 metres. In the centre, a fine marble pool with generously festooned edges reflects in its calm waters the image of the four iwans.

The visitor's attention is usually attracted first to the western iwan because of its sandy colour and the soberness of its decoration of small mosaic squares inlaid in the brick. The architecture of the apse is also different from that of the Safavid mosques: there are no pendentives or complicated stalactites to overload the vault which is made up of large alveoles of very pure design. This 18th century construction however is not the most remarkable.

The southern porch opens up on a very wide and elegant arch, the proportions of its architrave, which is wider than it is high, are perfect but unfortunately two minarets which were subsequently added detract from its harmony. This layout, which is relatively rare, reflects a "Mongol" influence; the porch was built under the Timurid dynasty (Tamerlane's) in the 15th century. The mosaics on its sides represent stars, rosettes, and very original stylized floral motifs. Generally speaking, blue shades predominate.

Jame' Mosque
Oljaitu's altar in Jame' Mosque

The small cupola - "Gonbad-e Khaki" (Brown Cupola) - which covers the northern hall has very elegant proportions and extremely fine decorations.

Isfahan, Jame' Mosque, Qibla Iwan, 15th to 17th centuries. Although the main construction of this iwan goes back to the twelfth century, the vaulting and the construction of the two minarets is late fifteenth century, while the inscriptions and part of the pediment were erected under the Safavids in the sixteenth and seventeenth centuries.

Isfahan, All Saviour's Cathedral (known as the Vank). Its design is very much that of the domed sanctuary chamber of a Persian mosque, with the addition of a raised chancel and altar within a semi, octagonal apse. By contrast to its modest exterior, the Cathedral's interior is lavishly decorated.

Madrasah Chahar Bagh

The most frequently visited madrasah in Isfahan is Chahar Bagh or Soltani formerly Madar-e Shah (Shah's Mother) situated at Chahar Bagh Avenues. This Koranic school was founded upon the initiative of Shah Soltan Hosain's mother. The Shah was the last of the Safavid sovereigns who, after taking refuge in this very building, was put to death by the Afghan invaders (1622). In order to finance the school, Hosain's mother got a large caravanserai built nearby, the income of which went to the Foundation. Nowadays there are only a few students in the madrasah, but the caravanserai has become the most famous luxury hotel in Iran.

The blue and gold flower-decked cupola flanked by two magnificent minarets can be photographed from the balconies of the hotel rooms. The same canal waters and cools the gardens where the hotel clients spend hot midday hours and the closed courtyard surrounded by high plane trees where generations of theologians meditated.

The madrasah was skilfully restored. The caravanserai, which became the Abbasi Hotel was almost entirely rebuilt. Its luxurious decorations are probably somewhat overdone. But in any case, it demonstrates the skill of contemporary artists such as glassworkers, sculptors on plaster, goldsmiths, carpet weavers or painters.

Chahar Bagh Madrasah

Isfahan, Chahar Bagh Madrasah formerly Madar-e Shah Madrasah. The last great building erected under the Safavids, it was built by Shah Soltan Hosain and dedicated to the Mother of the Shah. The central court, with its pool and garden, are surrounded by arcades on two levels, each giving access to a student's room. The arcades are broken by iwans, which were used as lecture halls.

The old caravanserai beside the Madrasah has become the most famous luxury hotel in Iran known as Abbasi Hotel.

Imam Mosque (Masjid-e Imam)

The Masjid-e Imam is one of the finest monuments in the world. The colour of the ceramic ornaments is the first cause of surprise and admiration. But the size of the buildings surrounding the main courtyard provokes a deeper emotion.

Like the builder of cathedrals, but using completely different means, the Muslim architect of the mosque used space and stone for mystical purposes. The first impression is one of completely unusual surroundings, the second a breathtaking reaction to the immensity and vacuum of the courtyard, the third a feeling of oppression provoked by this closed and silent world, the monotonous rectangle of arcades and loggias where minarets mount their blind guard and onto which the gaping dark mouths of the iwans open.

Man, alone with his God, seems minute in this decor, prostrate at the very limit of sun and shade, but even the pagan visitor's soul is gladdened by the monumental harmony.

Then comes the joy of discovering a thousand details: a turquoise ropemoulding underlining the ogive of an arcade, the magnificence of the lettering running along yards and yards of cornice, in some cases intricate interlacing, on others geometrically stylized; the complexity of the system of flying buttresses supporting the large iwans, which for once is visible (without having to climb on the roofs) from a delightfully flower-decked side courtyard.

Imam Mosque formely known as Masjid-e Shah or Royal Mosque

Imam Mosque, summer sanctuary

132

A general view of Naqsh-e Jahan Square (left), 17th century Royal Mosque (Imam Mosque), Sheikh Lotfollah Mosque 17th century.

Chehel Sotun (Forty columns)

The Chehel Sotun (Forty Columns) Palace is an even more striking example of the refinement of the Safavid Kings' courts. It is a charming pavilion in the heart of a park, at the far end of a long pool; it is supported by twenty wooden columns, and since these are reflected in the water, you have a palace with forty columns! Shah Abbas II and his successors received there dignitaries and ambassadors, either on the terrace or in one of the state reception halls.

Like in the Ali Qapu, the walls were covered with frescoes and paintings. They are damaged by old age, but are also being restored. They depict specific historical scenes such as a reception for an Uzbek King in 1646 when the palace had only just been completed; a banquet in honour of the King of Turkestan in 1611; the battle of Chalderan against the King of Osmanis in 1514 in which the Persians fought without fire-arms; the welcome extended to a Mongol King who took refuge in Iran in 1544; then battle of Taherabad in 1510 where the Safavid King Shah Isma'il vanquished and killed the Uzbek King. A sixth large painting, which is more recent, depicts Nader Shah's victory against the Indian army at Karnal, in 1747. There are also less anecdotic but prettier small mural compositions in the traditional miniature style, which celebrate the joy of living.

The superb wooden roof of the porch was painted with a series of geometrical decorations interspersed with flowers. The waterproofing of this, and other palaces, was achieved by covering the roof with a fresh layer of beaten earth every year, the weight of which has caused many others to collapse.

Chehel Sotun Palace, 17th century

Isfahan, Chehel Sotun, mid-17th century. This pavilion is one of several which used to adorn the gardens of the palace compound. The great porch rests on 20 wooden columns and leads into a central suite of rooms painted with historical scenes. The iwan behind the porch is lined with mirror mosaic.

Fresco, Chehel Sotun Palace, 17th century

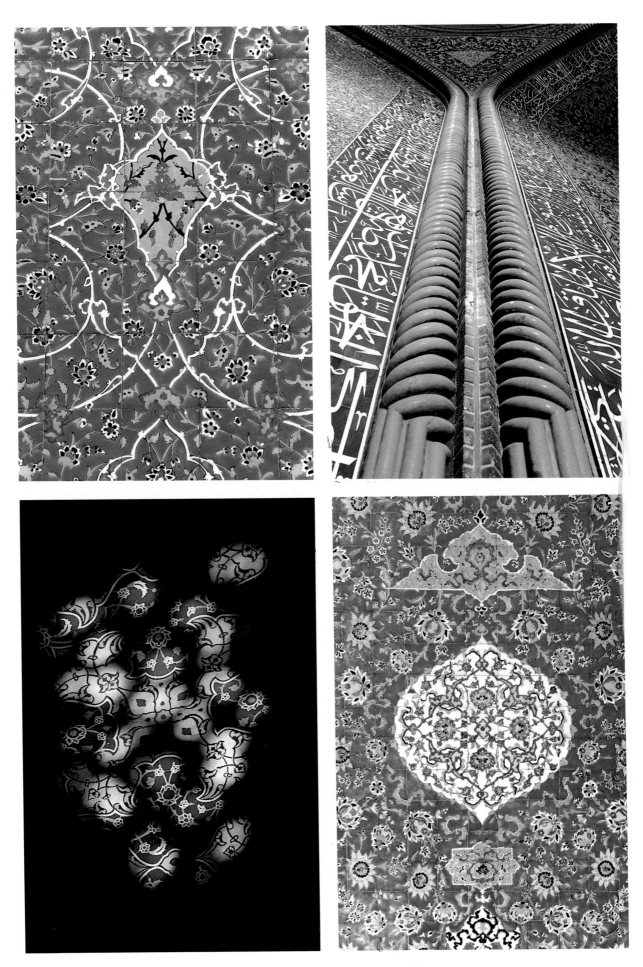

Isfahan, tileworks of Sheikh Lotfollah Mosque

139

The perfect cupola of Sheikh Lotfollah Mosque

This mosque differs from all others in several respects. While turquoise, blue and pink predominate in the motifs on the facade, elsewhere, especially on the dome, both inside and outside, the main colour is yellow. The artist painted on this background delicate interlacings and black or blue flowers.

The cupola is recognized as the most perfect in Iran. Uncanny lighting seeps through the windows at the base of the vault. Widespread use is made of the decorative value of

Portal and interior of Sheikh Lotfollah Mosque

calligraphy in the "sols" or "thulth" lettering style, but there are also realistic miniature-style motifs: flower-bowls, peacocks, cypresses, etc.

Another peculiarity of this mosque is that it has no courtyard nor minaret, since it was not a place for public worship, but was exclusively intended for the King, his family and his close collaborators.

Just after the madrasah and the entrance of the new bazaar, a high stone gateway leads into a park (which is private but open on certain occasions) which used to be for a long time one of the largest and most pleasant in 17th century Isfahan. It is called Bagh-e Bolbol, the "Nightingale Garden". In the centre of the trees and flowers, there is a charming pavilion with wooden columns, the Hasht Behesht.

Talar-e Ashraf (Royal Residence), ceiling decorations ▶

Isfahan, Ali Qapu, beginning 17th century. When Shah Abbas decided to move his capital to Isfahan there was already a small Timurid pavilion alongside what was to become the great square. This he converted into the Ali Qapu, the great gatehouse of the palace complex overlooking the square.

144

Isfahan, Ali Qapu, Music room, beginning 17th century. The entire upper floor of the palace gatehouse consists of a group of rooms whose walls are decorated with a fretwork of niches and bottle shapes cut into a wood and plaster membrane which lines the walls.

The construction of Harun Velayat or Harouniyeh in Isfahan is composed of a cupola, a tombbox, two courtyards and two portals beautifully ornamented with mosaic tiles. It was erected in (1512 A.D.), in the reign of Safavid monarch Shah Isma'il, and later repaired under other sovereigns of the same dynasty. Its tile-works have earned the monument a well-deserved place among Isfahan's historical remains.

146

A Coppersmith in Isfahan bazaar

attention: the Sareban (Camel Driver) Minaret. It juts out from the centre of a small square and rises 44 metres above the ground. On its upper portion, a double collar is reminiscent of the lotus flower capitals of the Karnak Columns. A discreet blue brick decoration underlines this motif, while the rest of the column is decorated with geometrical designs formed by the relief of bare bricks...

There are other noteworthy minarets in the areas to the west and south-west of the Friday Mosque. The double Dardasht Minarets reportedly date back to the Mongol period. Their bodies, which are now truncated, have an attractive spiralshaped dark blue faience decoration. They frame a semi-ruined portal and are near a beautiful bare earth cupola.

Further to the south at the entrance of the covered street of the bazaar, the Ali Mosque Minaret is the highest in Isfahan: 50 metres!

A little further south, there are two minarets on each side of a porch above the street. They are called Domenar Dar-ol Ziafeh.

As he leaves the Friday Mosque, the visitor can take a stroll along twisting streets in the cloth-trading area. Within a perimeter of 500 metres, there are minor buildings worthy of interest. First, to the north-east, two very high bare brick minarets dominating a populous area with very narrow streets difficult to negotiate by car.

The nearest minaret to Saghir Isfahani Avenue (to the right going up Hatef Avenue where you leave your car) is Menar-e Chehel Dokhtaran, the "Forty Girls Minaret". It is only 30 metres high. About 200 metres further on, a slimmer column of brick attracts your

The famous "Shaking Minarets": Menar Jonban (5 kilometres west via Sheikh Bahaei Avenue). Twin towers flank a porch with a very wide ogive. If you lean out of an embrasure at the top of the tower and sway your body regularly, the tower starts oscillating in a perfectly visible manner and soon the second minaret starts moving also. For a long time, this curious phenomenon was attributed to the magic powers of the holy priest buried under the iwan. Nowadays, it would be easy to calculate the physical stresses involved.

Isfahan, Menar Jonban (Shaking Minarets)

Isfahan, Ali Minaret, late 12th century. Nearly 48 metres high, this minaret is the tallest in Isfahan. The shaft bears patterns in brick and turquoise faience. An interesting feature is the use of cavetto cornices.

The oldest bridge (12th century) is about 7 km out of town downstream. It can be reached both from the left and right banks. The Shahrestan Bridge (named after a neighbouring village) is a fine arched bridge, slightly incurvated with arches of varying sizes. It is not open to traffic. The landscape is very peaceful with clumps of poplar-trees and pebbles rolling on the bed of the river, which is fast-running in this particular spot.

Isfahan, Pigeon Tower, 19th century. Looking like a series of medieval castles, hundreds of these towers dot the fields around Isfahan. The interiors are honeycombed with cells which provided a home to thousands of pigeons whose droppings were then collected once a year and spread on the fields to act as fertilizer for the superb melons which have always been the pride of the region.

Pir-e Bakran Mausoleum, (30 km from Isfahan) together with a gallery and a courtyard dating back to the 14th cent. A.D. was constructed in the reign of the Mongol II-Khan Oljaitu. This complex of structures bears two dates, (1303 and 1312 A.D.), and possesses excellent stucco decorations and tile-work inscriptions in Thulth and Kufic calligraphies. A series of inscriptional plasterworks add considerably to the grandeur and charm of this monument. The mausoleum is that of a 14th century pious man, Mohammad Ibn-e Bakran and consists of a gallery, a courtyard, a portal and the actual tomb. The name of the constructor and decorator of this superb building, given in the inscription, is Mohammad Naqqash (the painter), and his work ranks among the masterpieces of the decorative arts in Iran.

Kashan

Name: Also called Kachan.
Situation and access: Province of Isfahan altitude 1,600 metres. 260 km S of Tehran, via Qom (105 km) on a good road. 220 km N of Isfahan, via Natanz, on road and track. 250 km N.W. of Na'in, on road and track. Railway.

Kashan is the first of the large oases along the Qom-Kerman road which runs along the edge of the great desert. Its charm is therefore mainly due to the contrast between the parched immensities of the Kevir region and the greenery of the well-tended oasis, to the lively atmosphere of this almost compulsory halt, the restful shade of cupola — or vault — covered houses and the coolness of gardens made even more pleasant by their water-fountains. The caravansaries near the city are in ruins but Kashan's secular function remains.

Between Kashan and Fin, there is a mosque — mausoleum overlooked by cypress-trees, which serves as a dwelling-place for several families of carpet-weavers.

Nearby, a small museum contains a few fine long-beaked vases, a speciality of ancient Kashi craftsmen which later became popular throughout Persia.

In Kashan and in the neighbouring towns of Ravand and Natanz, a picturesque event draws large crowds each year during the month of Moharram. The audience participates enthusiastically in the three day-reconstitution of Hosain's "passion-play" as a great martyr of the Shi'ite faith. The argument of this was written by a Kashi poet at the end of the 16th century.

Aerial view of the city, Boroujerdiha Residence, 19th cent., Carpet sellers, Kashan Bazaar

152

Madrasah Soltani is one of the beautiful and famous structures of Kashan and dates from 19th cent. A. D. This Madrasah which resembles the Chahar Bagh and Sadr Madrasah in Isfahan in its structure, is extremely attractive for possessing a portal, a huge brick cupola, vast prayer halls, side-chambers, and beautiful tile-works.

Aqa Madrasah (theological school), one of the famous Madrasahs of the Qajar period is highly valuable for its architectural and construction techniques. Its huge cupola and two tile minarets are, at present, the tallest of the historical structures to be found in Kashan. The portal of the Madrasah bears an inscription composed by the poet Hasrat, which is set on tile in Nasta'liq script and dated (1851 A.D.).The huge brick cupola and the winter prayer halls are on the second floor and the beautiful courtyard of the edifice possess chambers.

An important religious ceremony held annually on the 21st day of Ramadan (fasting month), takes place in the historic site of Mohammad Helal Shrine in Aran, 10 km to the north of Kashan. Helal was a direct descendant of His Holiness Imam Ali.

The present premises of Kashan Cultural Heritage Department, the Boroujerdis' Old House was built nearly 130 years ago by a famous merchant and landowner named Haj Seyyed Ja'far Natanzi (later known as Boroujerdi family) from Natanz, who imported goods from Boroujerd in Lorestan province. The construction date (1293 A. H.) can still be seen on the covered inscription of the building, completion of which required 18 years of work by tens of labours, master painters, and architects.

The mausoleom of Shazdeh Ibrahim, built in 1894 A.D., belongs to the Qajar period. It is highly interesting and attractive for its turquoise tiled cupola, lofty minarets, a pleasant courtyard and an iwan decorated with mirror-works and paintings.

Founder of the edifice is a certain is a certain Khaleh Beigom, a citizen of Fin, buried inside the mausoleum, and on whose tombstone some verses have been carved in her praise as the benefactor of the endowment.

Kashan's water-supply comes from a system of qanats which converge up on the oasis. But the city also benefits from the presence nearby of an abundant spring which enabled King Shah Abbas the Great to create a blooming garden in the suburb of Fin. (6 km South). Bagh-e Fin, has its poetic appeal and gardeners are attempting to restore the luxuriance of flower-beds overlooked by century – old cypress–trees. Workmen are also restoring a pavilion where the Sovereign enjoyed the refined pleasures described by poets and illustrated by miniaturists.

Maranjab, the Great Kevir, central Iran ▶

Abyaneh

One of the most attractive to visit is in the village of Abyaneh, which was completely Zoroastrian right until the time of the intolerant Safavid Shah Isma'il I in whose reign most of the villagers emigrated to India or to Yazd. Even today their costume, way of life and ancient dialect are still practically unchanged.

Drive for about 42 km. to Dehji, along the road to Natanz, south of Kashan; a few km, further on, see a good gravel road to the west, before the Hinjan bridge, where a sign indicates Abyaneh and the magnificent Barzrud valley. Some 25 km. along this road, passing Hinjan village, you reach Abyaneh at the bottom of a gorge dominated by a small Mongol fort. The main

street goes right through the remains of the 'Atashkadeh' or temple, open on three sides and with a broken dome.

About 300 m from the Atashkadeh, on the same lane, is an interesting mosque with a probably Safavid entrance and corridor, and next to it, below the present building, another mosque believed to be pre-Seljuq, with an exceptionally beautiful and unusual carved wooden mihrab protected by a sheet of glass.

Tile-works of Sheikh Abd-ol Samad in Natanz with a fine calligraphic band in Kufic inscription, 14th cent.

Natanz is a small mountain town located forty-nine miles from Kashan, famed for its bracing climate and fruit orchards. Vulture mountain looms over the town, and local residents point in its direction telling how the troops of Alexander killed the Achaemenian King, Darius III, nearby. Many small shrines dot the mountainside like this Imamzadeh suspended in the mist of a spring morning.

Natanz, Shrine of "Abd-ol Samad" 14th century. The elements in the present complex date from 1304 with subsequent additions and restorations; the lofty minaret is dated 1325. The pyramidal roof is over the tomb of the Sheikh which is dated 1307.

Na'in

Name: Also called Naein, Naiyin ... .
Situation and access: Province of Isfahan. Altitude 1,400 metres. 150 km E of Isfahan, on a good road, 180 km N-E of Yazd on a somewhat deteriorated asphalted road, 510 km S of Tehran on road and track via Qom (355 km), Kashan (250 km).

Half-way between Isfahan and Yazd, this mall town which has the colour of the earth around it, formerly a caravan cross –roads, seems asleep amidst a desert of stones which appears endless whichever the direction from which you approach the town. It is however worth a halt for the sake of a visit to three buildings. The magnificent varnished brick cupolas of two of these are visible from the roadside. But there are no two cupolas alike nor two identical blues....

One of the domes in Na'in, a very ancient one, is blue and white; the other, emerald green and yellow, looks as if it were built yesterday. The first one covers a classical Imamzadeh preceded by a small inside courtyard where a few old men are fingering their prayer-beads. The second one overlooks an octagonal brick tomb in the centre of a shady pine and fruit-tree garden where students read and write, sitting on a step far from the crowds and noise.

The third monument in Na'in is the inevitable "Friday Mosque", " Masjed-e Jom'eh" (to the east of the city by the Anarak road). It is not richly decorated: it has a bare brick cupola and a curious octagonal pointed minaret. Inside, austerity reigns: there is neither faience nor an iwan. The latter architectural structure, a typically Iranian one developed at the end of the 11th century while the Na'in Mosque was built before that date, at the very start of Islamization. It was rebuilt in 960 and is one of the most ancient in the whole of Iran. Formerly an important halt on the road to the East through the Great Desert (the famous «silk road»), Na'in's main activity today is that of its carpet-makers said to be the most skilful in the whole of Iran.

Aerial view of Na'in, water reservoir and interior of Jame' Mosque.

Pirnia Residence, interior design, Na'in

Zavareh, Jame' Mosque, iwan and arcade, 1135 A.H. This fine example of an early four-iwan mosque is situated in an oasis town on the edge of the central Iranian desert. The plain brick arcades of its courtyard are highlighted by a simple monumental inscription while the interior arcading of the dome chamber is ornamented with carved stucco panels and a superb stucco mihrab.

Ardestan, Jame' Mosque, detail, 12th century. Adjacent to the dome chamber, the soffit of this arch is decorated with an inscription which is in an excellent state of preservation.

Kerman Province

Name: In old Persian Beh Ardeshir (named after the Sassanid King Ardeshir I, founder of the town), subsequently Bardesir . Situation and access: Provincial capital. Altitude 1,860 metres. 370 km to the S-E of Yazd, 800 km from Isfahan by a good asphalt road. 500 km to the N of Bandar Abbas by excellent road. 520 km to the, W. of Zahedan, by a newly-built road as far as Bam (200 km), thereafter road under repair.

Eight to nine hours by motorcar by an asphalt road will get you from Isfahan to Kerman. Also, daily flights by Iran Air are linking up that provincial capital with Tehran as well as with the principal townships of the south of Iran.

The distance covered between airport and town centre provides a first assessment of the size and recent expansion of Kerman. Wide, twin carriageway avenues, adorned with flowering shrubs and fountains, are jutting out far beyond the confines of the built-up area.

Being a town of considerable past history, Kerman is not looking to the future only. Its people are proud of several ancient monuments of particular originality, among them a group of utilitarian buildings dating from the Safavid period in the 17th century.

They are centred on a large arcaded square where in days bygone the caravans used to come to a halt. Each side of it is flanked by buildings having their own particular purpose — such as the caravanserai proper with its apartments and warehouses; the workshops reserved for the artisans of the bazaar, mostly coppersmiths; huge cisterns which had been in operation up till a short while ago.

There are two more excursions which are a must for everyone visiting Kerman — inspecting the dead city of Bam and the dervishes' sanctuary at Mahan (40 km out of Kerman on the Bam road), both of which can be done in one day.

Tile-works of Hammam-e Ganj Ali Khan, Shah Ne'matollah Mausoleum, a *kobeh* (door-knock), all in Kerman.

Kerman, Jabal-e Sang. Meaning "Mountain of Stone", this domed chamber is one of the most majestic monuments of southern Iran and one of the most puzzling. Neither its date nor use can be determined with certainty, but it probably dates from the late twelfth century and was possibly never finished.

A 17th century Hammam turned museum

The public baths, disused as such and converted to serve as a museum. It is the most interesting sight for visitors, known as the Hammam Ganjali Khan (named after a former governor of the province). The principal doorway is adorned with murals depicting animal scenes. The staggered entrance gives access to a first chamber surrounded by six spacious apses. Close to a pool for first ablutions bathers could undress and have a rest.

Thence narrow passages led to a row of dome-covered halls, each of which served a particular purpose, such as massages, hot and cold baths, etc. True-to-life wax figures bring back the memory of everyday scenes of the past. All garments and other objects exhibited are period pieces — razors, sandals, phials for attar of roses, pipes with small bowls and long stems to be enjoyed after the bath. They are, incidentally, very much like the similar objects used in the hammams of today. A little further to the north, another hammam — similar but dating from the 18th century only — is still in operation. It is, like the madrasah next door, named after another provincial governor, Ibrahim Khan. From one of the short sides of the great square opens the access to the Vakil Bazaar. Its vaulted gallery offers a handsome example of the craftsmanship of Iranian bricklayers.

The way the cupolas rest on their pilasters reflects a consummate mastery of architecture.

Waxed statue in Ganjali Khan Bath, Kerman bazaar

171

Bam, in the Kerman province. The abandoned city, the forgotten fortress, the extinct caravanserai form a gigantic abstract composition of the same colour as the earth and desert around it.

Bam

Situation and access: Kerman Province. Altitude 1,000 m 190 km S-E of Kerman by excellent road. 330 km W of Zahedan by track (road under construction). Auxiliary airfield. Iran Air flights via Kerman.

There is not much to say about Bam. What could one tell about a dead city, a funereal town, of which it is thought wise to lock the unique, heavy gate for the night so that no human being nor even animal could disturb its secular silence, nor violate its homesteads, forever in ruins?

Four concentric enclosures

A first association of ideas brings back names such as Avila and Carcassonne with their impenetrable belts of ramparts; Les Baux, for the wind lashing its walls; Pompei breathing death and destruction... But what's the good of similes? Bam is a city moulded in the red clay of the Great Iranian Desert. Typically Iranian are its sharply pointed, broken arches, its flamboyant domes, its tapering towers and its walled enclosure so broadly based on a soil not reputed for its solidity.

More than three kilometres is the length of the crenellated walls, supported by dozens of towers for the defense of the ancient city. Inside, a triple ring of fortifications protects the citadel perched on top of a hill. From its keep, overlooking an impenetrable mountain range to the south and the endless desert to the north, can be seen that route of trade and invasions which the Sassanid Kings already had wished to control. Subsequently the Arabs extended their sway over it, only to be superseded by the Seljuq Turks in the 11th century. In the end it was the Afghans who, with their devastating raid, in 1722, which carried them as far as Isfahan, dealt the fatal blow to the fortress of Bam, as well as to that of Kerman (see section under this heading). The total abandonment of the old city is, however, probably of a more recent date, otherwise its ruins would be in a much more dilapidated state.

Shah Ne'matollah Vali (mystic sufi) Mausoleum, Mahan (17th century)

Mahan, the most beautiful minarets of Iran

Generally speaking, tourists arriving in the south of Iran have already had the opportunity to admire many a fine building: their enthusiasm therefore tends to get blunted. All the greater will be their surprise on beholding the sights of Mahan.

A faience tiled dome combined with crude brick cupolas; four tall minarets, lantern-shaped at the top, the whole set in a cluster of trees.

The building, set in a jewel-box of greenery, stands out against a back ground of violet-coloured mountains crowned with snow. The blue of the dome mingles with the dark blue of the sky, the sky of the Iranian desert at the altitude of 2,000 metres. The twin minarets are covered with turquoise tiles, from the bottom up right to the bulbous cupola; the lantern, topped by eight stocky pillars, is entirely covered by blue faience tiles.

Within this sanctuary is the tomb of a saintly person, said to have lived for a hundred years, from 1331 to 1431: Shah Nur-ed Din, Ne'matollah Vali, poet, sage, sufi and founder of an order of dervishes. To this day they are numerous in Iran and they meet in the sanctuary of Mahan. The roots of the philosophy they practise reach back to the time of the Achaemenians, to the days of Cyrus. To them life means being uprooted; their striving is for the return through death to their "native land". With it all they have no contempt for this world of transition, but in order to make sure that they will be able to return to their source of origin they have to work their passage home with their activities, their patience and their tolerance... All this is the typical Iranian wisdom.

The tomb and the great assembly hall next to it do not present any particular decoration, except for the ceiling which one could easily take for a Kerman rug.

Mausoleum of Shah na'matollah Vali

Bagh-e Shazdeh, 19th century, Mahan

Kermanshah Province
Bisotun

Situation and access: Provincial capital, Kurdestan region. Altitude 1,630 metres. 200 km E of Khosrawi (Iraq / Iran border). 390 km of Baghdad on a good road. 590 km S-W of Tehran, via Hamedan (190 km) on a good road. 605 km S of Tabriz on a good road and 80 km of track, via Sanandaj (160 km). 750 km N of Abadan on a very good road.

Like Hamedan, Kermanshah is on the age-old Asia-Mediterranean caravan route, and similarly was many times rebuilt. There is only one vestige, but it is a remarkable one, the Taq-e Bostan, "the Garden Arch" (3 km north). It is a group of rock sculptures, several of them protected by a porch roof which forms a grotto. (Better visited during the afternoon). Rupestral motifs date back to the great Sassanid period (3rd century A.D. until Islam). The bas-relief on the right shows the investiture of Ardeshir II(379); the King receives from God Hormozd a ribbon-decked ring, the symbol of royal power; to his right God Mithra holds a bunch of sacred branches, a ritual instrument in use since the Median period.

From Kermanshah the road runs along the bottom of a fine velvety fawncoloured cliff. Bisotun clusters around a source nearby a vertical rock wall. On the roadside there are inscriptions engraved in the rock in three languages (ancient Persian, Elamite, Akkadian or neo-Babylonian). This enabled British officer Rawlinson to decipher Babylonian. The inscriptions tell the story of the battles Darius had to wage in 521-520 B.C. against the governors who were trying to dismantle the empire founded by Cyrus. The nineteenth, decisive, victory took place on this site. A bas-relief portrays this exploit; unfortunately the scene showing the King with his principal enemy at his feet and eight rebel governors enchained behind him is some 50 metres above ground level and is hardly visible without the use of binoculars.

Sassanian bas-relief in Taq-e Bostan, Parthian temple at Kangavar, all in Kermanshah

Sassanian bas-relief, 7th century, Taq-e Bostan, Kermanshah

178

The victory of Darius II over rebels, Bisotun, Kermanshah

This provincial capital is developing rapidly (refinery and miscellaneous industries). It is a lively market-centre for southern Kurdestan (the north prefers to shop in Sanandaj). You therefore meet there a large number of Kurds, mountain peasants famous as warriors, reputedly somewhat mysterious due to their tumultuous history.

The Kurds still speak their own language among themselves and remain faithful to their vestimentary traditions: they wear large turbans on their heads and black dungarees tight at the waist and at the ankles which make them look as if they had just stepped out of a combat tank. The women wear trousers and bright-coloured scarves. Despite their unusual clothes, their fiery eyes and large moustaches, the Kurds are very sociable.

The surroundings of Taq-e Bostan: ochre cliffs, a small water-pool, a flower-decked garden decorated with antique stones enhances the attractiveness of this remarkable archaeological site.

Recently installed hotel facilities make Kermanshah a suitable halt on the Baghdad-Tehran or Tabriz - Isfahan routes via the Kurdestan region.

On the outskirts you should see Bisotun and in the direction of Iraq, two ancient sites: 3 km from Sar-e Pol-e Zahab, a Median tomb (7th century B.C.) called Dokkan-e Davoud, "David's shop", and near the same village, bas-reliefs dating back to the Akkadians, i.e. 2300 years B.C. But even more than by these ancient vestiges, the traveller will be charmed around Kermanshah (especially on the Sanandaj road) by the beauty of the landscapes in which the rough and the mellow combine harmoniously.

The village of Harsin (30 km to the s) lies within the archaeological site where the "Lorestan bronzes" were discovered. Most of these magnificent objects, known all over the world, are on display at the Tehran Archaeological Museum.

Mausoleum of Baba Yadegar, Tekiyeh Mo'aven- ol Molk, Kermanshah

Khorasan Province
Mashhad

Situation and access: Provincial capital of Khorasan. Altitude 970 metres. 875 km E of Tehran on road and track, via Shahrud, Sabzevar (225 km), Naishabour (110 km), or 1,335 km on track and northern road, via Gorgan (925 km), Bojnurd (280 km), Qushan (145 km), 1,350 km N-E of Isfahan on road and track through the Great Desert, via Na'in (1,190 km), Tabas (604 km), Gonabad (300 km). 1,000 km N of Zahedan, on track via Birjand (500 km), 220 km N-W of Taibad (20 km) after the Iran — Afghanistan frontier, on road and track. International Airport and services to Tehran, Zahedan. Railway: liaison with Tehran by turbotrain.

Astan-e Qods, "The sacred threshold"

On approaching the airport, the plane from Tehran usually makes a complete circle around the town. Long parallel, star-shaped, concentric avenues run through this very large centre surrounded by greenery. But the most important is a ring in the east of the city surrounding a complex system of buildings and courtyards dominated by a turquoise blue cupola and another golden one which glitters in the sun. This glimpse from an altitude of 200 metres is the only one a miscreant can hope to get of the sacred enclosure of Mashhad.

Once on the ground, he is fascinated by the golden cupolas and minarets but non-Moslems are not allowed through the Astan-e Qods, the "Sacred Threshold". Here lies the tomb of Shi'ite Islam's most venerated saint: Imam Reza, the Eighth Imam assassinated in 817

Heart of the city and pilgrims' domain

The tourist sees the floors of the sanctuaries and of its porticos as paved with marble and covered with sumptuous carpets but the believers see Archangel Gabriel spreading his wings under the feet of the pilgrims..."

The visitor should circle the forbidden area at different times of the day, to observe the processions and the ebb and flow of the crowds. He will note the variety of types which come from all parts of Iran and even from beyond its frontiers, with a majority of nomads from the south and mountain-dwellers from Afghanistan; some distinctly Mongol types are also distinguishable.

The entrance and tomb of Imam Reza's Holy shrine, Mashhad.

In A.D. 817 the Caliph Ma'mun, the son of Haroun Al-Rashid, while travelling from Merv to Baghdad in company with Ali Al-Reza, the eighth of the Shi'a Imams, halted for a few days in a village on the site of Mashhad, sixteen miles to the south/east of the large city of Tus. Whilst there, the Imam partook too freely of grapes and died almost immediately; the suddenness of his death led to the suspicion that the Caliph had poisoned him. Ali Al-Reza was buried where he died, and his tomb soon became a place of pilgrimage; the village that grew around this tomb was called Mashhad, meaning " the place of martyrdom ". Being much exposed to attack by the wild tribes of Central Asia and Afghanistan, Mashhad experienced many vicissitudes in after years, but, although the shrine of the Imam suffered greatly on more than one occasion, its sanctity steadily increased, and it became the holiest spot in Persia. By the destruction of Tus in 1389 by one of Tamerlane's sons, Mashhad benefited, as many of the survivors of the stricken city settled there. In the early fifteenth century Shahrokh, Tamerlane's son and successor, often visited Mashhad, and his pious wife Gowhar Shad built the beautiful mosque adjoining the shrine of the Imam which bears her name.

Nader Shah (1736-47), after making Mashhad his capital, endowed the shrine with the magnificent gilded portico and a minaret that was also covered with gold. Early in the following country Fath Ali Shah constructed the New Court of the shrine, and he and his great grandson Naser-od Din Shah (1848-96) founded a number of religious colleges in the town.

To the visitor, a mosque evokes a palace with fabulous decorations but in the eyes of the believer, these temples continue to be, above all, a place appropriate for worship and prayer.

Khwajeh Rabi' Mausoleum, king Nader Tomb an old Naderi Fortification, 18th century, all in Khorasan

Belqais city, northern Khorasan, Kalat– e Naderi, Tomb of Hakim Mo'men in the centre of Mashhad

Nader Shah the Brave's capital

The museum is the only enclave where tourists may penetrate the forbidden circle. You discover there some valuable objects: a 1.50 metre diameter stone crater entirely decorated with sculptured motifs of Mongol inspiration (1201), many prayer carpets woven with gold and silver threads, beautifully engraved gold string-courses, several very rare Korans including some in Kufic characters which date back to the early days of the Hegira.

The Nader Shah Mausoleum is a curious piece of architecture completed during the past few years, consisting in a heavy slab of concrete which forms a crypt and of a colossal bronze group representing soldiers led to battle by a sort of Carolus Magnus on horseback bearing a turban and a large axe. The composition does not lack movement. The crypt shelters the tomb of Nader Shah, who made Mashhad his capital and his operational base for his campaign against India. Two small museums have been set up nearby: Nader Shah's souvenirs, mainly 18th and 19th century weapons, and bronze objects uncovered during excavations in the region.

Mausoleum of Besh Qardash (five brothers),
Nader Tomb, Hakim Mo'men Mausoleum.

Khwaf Windmills, Nashtifan

Tus – Now called Ferdowsi (30 km. N-W of Mashhad). It was, long before Mashhad, a powerful city , but then the Mongols came… A ridge of clay running through the plain is all that is left of its ramparts . the size which give an indication of how large a city it was. Ferdowsi. " the Homer of Iran" was born there. He has buried under a mausoleum built about fifty years ago. The massive appearance of the monument is lightened by a flower – decked the monument is lightened by a flower- decked garden with a water- pool.

Tomb of Ferdowsi, and Interior of Tus Museum

Sweet melon of Mashhad, a Mashhadi dyer,
Radkan Tomb-tower, 12th century

Radkan (80 km N-W of Mashhad on the Quchan road): very fine Mongol funeral tower with conical roof and grooved brickwork.

Zoshk (35 km W of Mashhad): a village perched on a hill in a hilly wooden region with small, rivers running through it, an exceptional kind of site for Iran.

Taibad (210 km S-E of Mashhad, near the Afghan frontier): Sheikh Zein-od Din Mausoleum, decorated with very fine coloured brick compositions of a style which one could call "modern".

The crafts of Khorasan are all represented in the bazaar. You should also visit a workshop were turquoises from the Naishabeur mines are cut and polished.

Naishabour (130 km W of Mashhad); a very fine monument built in 1934 on the tomb of the great poet Omar Khayyam who died in 1125; mausoleums in honour of Sheikh Attar, another great Persian poet who died in 1221 and of Mahruq, apostle of Islam. These buildings are surrounded by beautiful gardens. One can also visit turquoise-cutting workshops at Naishabour.

The mausoleum of Kamal-ol Molk Iranian famous painter is adjacent to that of Sheikh Attar in an attractive garden just outside Naishabour

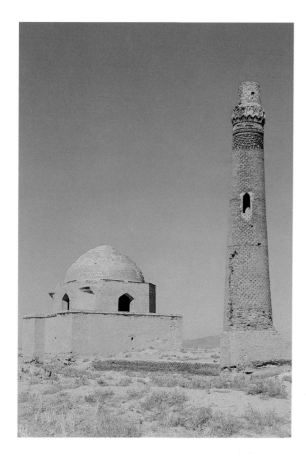

Sangbast Mausoleum, Mashhad. Tomb of Attar (mystic sufi) and Khayyam, the Great Iranian poet in Naishabour

Khosrowgerd Minaret in Sabzevar

Khuzestan Province
Shush/susa

Name:The French name Suse is frequently employed. Also called Shoosh, Chouch, etc... Situation and access: Khuzestan Province. Altitude 300 metres, 215 km N of Abadan, via Ahvaz (85 km). 1,000 km S-W of Tehran. 510 km S-E of Khosravi (Iran-Iraq frontier). 700 km of Baghdad. Good roads. Ahvaz airport.

There is no treasure in the sense of jewels or adornings. On the spot, the site is very disappointing for those who seek fine ruins. In this curious antique city there is not a single column standing (there are plans to restore some). There are only foundations, disembedded tambours and piles of clay marking the outline of the palace which Darius got built at Elam, his capital. But a lucky thrust of a spade on December 24th 1972 unearthed the statue, the first one of an Achaemenian King ever to be discovered.

Engravings on its base soon revealed that it was Darius himself. The inscription reads: "This is the stone statue that King Darius got made in Egypt so that those who saw it should know that the Persian has conquered Egypt".

Tomb of Daniel and a young man from Shushtar

The statue is 2.50 metres high. Unfortunately the head is missing, but archaeologists still hope to find it. Did they not two years earlier discover grey marble tablets with cuneiform characters engraved upon them? They were the foundation documents of Darius's palace. Buried under the walls, they contain an account of how it was built, of how cedar wood was brought from Lebanon, teak wood from Gandara, stone from Hapiratush, gold from Sardes and Bactres, ivory from Kush and from India. But even if this palace had been handed down to us, Susa's main interest would still be elsewhere.

Thirteen superimposed cities have been found here and this is why the site has such scientific importance. A stratigraphic section has been cut into the central hill ("tell") which is called the "Royal City". This has enabled scientists to recapture 4000 years of history. And here history can literally be read: during these 4000 years, fifteen languages and as many systems of writing were utilized in Susa. Small minutely engraved clay bricks or tablets which look like overcooked cakes are among the most ancient testimonies of the transcription of thought by conventional signs.

The alabaster receptacles and very delicate figurines date back to 3000 years B.C. and so does a bathtubshaped black stone sarcophagus. Bitumen weights and receptacles were made as "recently" as 2000 years B.C.; as for the clay horsemen bearing shields discovered in 1971, they only date back to the Parthian era... almost contemporary!The walls are adorned with castings (alas!) of the famous polychrome enamelled brick panels, the originals of which are in the Tehran Museum (as well as the also famous Lorestan bronzes) and in the Louvre, in Paris.

Susa is not only an archaeological site, it is also a village, a very lively one because of the devotion of the Shi'ites for the Prophet Daniel. The presumed tomb of the prophet (but there is a controversy on whether it is really the Daniel of the Bible) is marked by a strange white stone cone which is neither regular nor symmetric. A visit to Susa is not complete without an excursion to the Chogha Zanbil `Ziggurat'.

Chogha Zanbil Temple, Khuzestan Province. The largest man-made structure in Iran is the ziggurat of Chogha Zanbil built about 1250B.C. by the Elamite king, Untash–Gal, as the focal point of his pilgrimage and ceremonial center of Dur Untashi. This massive temple and tomb complex, located eighteen miles southeast of Shush (Susa), recreates on the flat plain the traditional awe man has always had for the mountain as a sacred place.

Abadan Port, cargo vessels, southwest of Iran

Mazandaran Province
Chalus

Name:Also called Chalus, Tchalous, etc. Situation and access: Mazandaran Province. On the Caspian Sea. Altitude 20 metres. 200 km N of Tehran via Karaj on a good twisting road. 80 km W of Ramsar, 120 km W of Babolsar on a coast road. Air port at Ramsar.

For the inhabitants of Tehran, Chalus is a seaside resort only three hours away from the capital. A seaside resort with forests and greenery! For the foreign tourist its contrast is surprising. There is also a beautiful mountain road with deep gorges, an artificial lake and the possibility of excursions in the Alam Kuh, the highest mountain complex in the Alborz range.

The coast itself is rather disappointing. A wall of sand-dunes hides the sea. Small concrete-block walls often prevent access to the beach. There are rows of ugly individual water-tanks perched on metallic structures. Villas of a questionable taste, painted in loud colours, are side by side with pretentious hotels.

There is a beautiful hinterland with wooden houses, granaries mounted on piles, fields which are green or golden according to the season, cow herds and horses running free, rows of trees which come as a surprise for those arriving from the plateau and the nearby bluetinged mountain-peaks.

You should not hesitate to leave the coastal road and take one of the tracks leading to small villages with an attractive rural population.

Chalus beach on the road to the north, Karaj Freeway

Tonekabon nature, Mazandaran Province

Ramsar

Situation and access: Mazandaran Province. Caspian resort, western part. Altitude 20 metres, 280 km N-W of Tehran via Chalus (80 km) on a picturesque hilly road, closed part of the winter, or 450 km via Qazvin and Rasht on an excellent road, usually open throughout the year. Airport, regular Iran Air services to Tehran and Rasht.

It is the bathing resort of the Caspian, and by far the most beautiful site of the whole coast. Wooded hills roll down nearly to the beach itself while the powerful outlines of the Alborz mountain range form an impressive background. The thin coastal strip is covered with rich vegetation including palm and orange-trees among the flower-beds.

Ramsar's two luxury hotels are set on two neighbouring terraces looking out upon a restful landscape. The oldest hotel has old-fashioned charm: extraordinary cast-iron statues covered with aluminium paint produce a wildly rococo effect. The new hotel forms a large white splash amidst the greenery. A long alley of palm-trees leads from the hotels to the beach.

Towards Chalus the forest sweeps right down to the sea. Large picnic sites have been organized under the oaks and elms.

View of **Ramsar and its luxury Hotel**

Marzanabad nature, Mazandaran Province

Qom Province

Name: Also called Qhom, Qum, and kumm, etc. Abbreviation for Kumandan (pre-Islamic). Situation and access: Central Province. Altitude, 1,600 metres. 155 km S of Tehran, hilly. 255 km N of Isfahan on a good road up to Neizar or 320 km via Kashan (105 km) on road and track. 320 km E of Hamedan on a good road except for a thirty-kilometre-passage. Railway: Tehran - Khorramshahr line.

The presence of an Iranian friend can greatly facilitate contacts and help you discover this unusual city.

Activities in Qom are concentrated on the sanctuary. You are struck from afar by a golden dome, powerful minarets like fortification towers and a large cupola covered with blue "tiles" decorated with foliated scrolls.

The sanctuary looks like a fortress in the material sense of the term, with high walls and immense portals better defended by compact semifanatic crowds than by any drawbridge or armed guards. In the evening, activities reach a peak before the tiredest pilgrims lie down for a brief sleep in the nook of a wall. Through wide-open doors, one catches a glimpse of an incredible collection of showy and glittering ornamentations, gold plate, mirror marquetry, coloured ceramics and thousands of bulbs and candles contribute to collective entrancement.

Like in Mashhad, the main attraction for tourists, rather than decoration and architecture, lies in the behaviour of the crowd of humble pilgrims for whom the journey is the achievement of the dream of a whole life, that of the dignified mollahs with their white turbans and fine linen clothes, that finally of small merchants who sell thousands of candles and prayer-beads, but also offer hideous vases, piles of pomegranates and delicious sweets made with honey.

The Awid river, which often runs dry, forms the northern limit of the city. Its waters run to waste in large depressions bordering the Great Desert.

Views of Qom and two tomb-towers near Qom

Qazvin Province

Name: Also called Kaswin, etc. Situation and access: Altitude 1,800 metres. 130 km N-W of Tehran on motorway and road (motorway planned). 520 km S-E of Tabriz on a good road. 210 km N-E of Hamedan on a good road. 250 km S of Bandar-e Anzali, 320 km S of Ramsar on a good but twisting road. Railway: Tehran - Tabriz line.

In September, the peasants lay bunches of grapes over hectares of land all over the fields. Many people travelling by car tend to drive through this long built-up area without even stopping. They are wrong. The covered bazaar is extremely lively: there are carpets, painted wood objects and antiquities... Two or three buildings justify a halt on the way to Tabriz, the Caspian or Hamedan, and can even be the goal of a special excursion from Tehran (1 hour 1/2 on an excellent road).

The Friday Mosque has been somewhat battered by earthquakes. It illustrates the difference of quality between Seljuq art (12th century, exterior decoration of the cupola, double string-course of Kufic writing inside) and the affectation of the Qajar period (19th century, minarets and iwans on the opposite side of the courtyard).

300 metres further south, at the bottom of a perspective of water-fountains, flower-beds and plane-trees, there is a magnificent blue cupola preceded by a portal with six small minarets, in the best baroque style. It is Imamzadeh Hosain. Hosain was Imam Reza's son.

Near the bazaar the Imam's Mosque, also a 19th century creation, although less delicate, will remind you of the mosques of Shiraz because of its ceramic floral decorations.

Shazdeh Hosain Mausoleum, Tekyieh Amini, Haidariyeh Madrasah (13th cent.)

Other monuments encountered as one strolls through the streets include the madrasah Haidariyeh, geographer Mostowfi's Mausoleum (east of the town), an abandoned madrasah occupied by pioneer squatters (west of the town) and public reservoirs reached through wide staircases descending eight or ten metres below ground-level.

Hashashin Castle

Those who favour ambitious excursions and unusual historical episodes should hire a guide and a Jeep to go near the source of the Alamut river in the heart of the Alborz mountain range (allow one full day for the return journey).

There, fortified eagles' nests recall unbelievable but authentic adventures of the "old man of the mountain" and of his sect of "Assassins" or "Hashashin" (drunk with hashish) which spread terror during the 12th century.

(The track leading to Alamut turns off to the left of the Tehran road, about 25 km from Qazvin).

Manjil Dam

Another highly recommended and less energetic excursion, even if you do not pursue it as far as the Caspian Sea, consists in a visit to the Manjil Dam.

Eighty kilometres from Qazvin, you cross the river near a picturesque old bridge: Pol-e Lowshan. Ten kilometres further on, you suddenly discover a turquoise blue lake set amidst mountains which are snow-covered until the beginning of April.

You can see the dam in the perspective of the valley looking toward the village of Manjil. Further down-stream Rudbar announces the pleasant Gilan region with its square houses with metal roofs scattered among the olive-and poplar-trees on the slopes of the valley.

Chehel Sotun museum and Shazdeh Hosain mausoleum in Qazvin.

Semnan Province

Name: In Old Persian Qoomes. Situation and access: Provincial capital. Altitude 1100 metres. 218 km to S-W of Tehran, 63 km to the S-W of Damghan by a good asphalt road.

Three to four hours by motorcar by an asphalt road will get you from Tehran to Semnan. Semnan has three cities named Shahrud, Damghan and Garmsar. It is bounded on the west by Ray and Tehran cities, on the east by Damghan, on the north by Gorgan and Sari cities and on the south by central Desert. It is said that Semnan was of the main provinces of ancient Iran. Its inhabitants speak in a specific language which seems to be one of the ancient Persian dialects. The Seljuqian minaret with an epitaph in Kufic script on it and the Friday Mosque beside the minaret are of the valuable monuments of Semnan.

The brick pattern on the minaret, Semnan, Jame' Mosque

Shahrud, which is 400 km far from Tehran, is abundant in fertile lands and orchards. The ancient city of Bastam, located 3km north-east of Shahrud, includes the tomb of Bayazid Bastami. Damghan is the other city of Semnan Province with a 6000-years old history. The mausoleum of Pir-e Alamdar and the minaret of Tari - Khaneh Mosque can be named of its famous monuments.

Jame' Mosque Bastam

An old entrance gate, 19th cent., Semnan

Tile works of Soltani Mosque, Semnan•

Interior design of Soltani Mosque

Bayazid-e Bastami and Jame' Mosque, Bastam

Sistan Province
Zabol

Situation and access: Province of Sistan. Altitude 1,300 metres. 210 km N-E of Zahedan on track. Zahedan airport, Iran Air services to Kerman, Mashhad.

The Sistan region is no doubt the most impenetrable but also the strangest in the whole of Iran. It is at the same time the paradise and the inferno of archaeologists. Formerly a sort of enchanted garden, celebrated by poets, and the seat of a refined civilization, the tumult of history has now turned it into an almost deserted countryside which houses fascinating vestiges.

Zabol is its capital which can be reached from Zahedan on a 230-kilometre track which is particularly trying in summer. The Sistan region forms a vast bowl with several lakes in its centre into which real rivers run including the enormous Hilmand river which comes down from the heart of Afghanistan.

On dry land, where one occasionally sees wheat fields, sesame, cotton and melons, alongside arid steppes, there are a large number of ruins. The visitor will particularly remember the dead city and striking Parthian citadel of Kuh-e Khwajeh. Archaeologists of various nationalities struggle to survive there because, in the Sistan region, the average summer temperature is 50 degrees centigrade and in winter it easily drops to 20 degrees below zero.

Also swept by wicked icy winds, this region which in antiquity was called Drangiane, the country of the legendary hero Rostam, has everything needed to attract curious minded tourists, and also to make them hesitate.

Bandar-e Chabahar, maritime gateway into Baluchestan, near the Pakistan frontier remember World War II when convoys of lorries from the besieged Soviet Union previous came to pick up material unloaded from allied ships.

Repair work is under way in the port, and the long road toward Zahedan — Mashhad is being modernized.

Thus even the most remote regions are participating in Iran's fabulous development effort and are benefitting from the nation's economic expansion.

This does not prevent hundreds of kilometres of this rocky and hilly coastline with its deep bays and many islands from remaining a natural reserve which will undoubtedly enchant tourists who are fond of sports, solitude, sunshine and deep-sea fishing in warm fish-strewn waters.

In the hinterland, palm oases can become interesting bases for winter vacations.

And out at sea, civilian and military hovercrafts, the largest tankers in the world and still-present antique-style Arab sailing boats never cease to plough the waves...

A Baluchi man, Jame' Mosque, Zabol, southeast of Iran

A Zaboli girl, southeast of Iran

Tehran Province

Name: Frequently written Tehran and more rarely, Tehrun.
Situation and access: Altitude between 1,200 and 1,700 metres. Mehrabad Airport to the west of city. Railway: European link through Tabriz and Istanbul, internal lines to Mashhad, Yazd and Khoramshahr. Regular coach services in all directions.

Nearly 12 million dwellers as against only two hundred thousand in 1920! Tehran is immense and proliferates like a coral reef, but in an orderly manner. Nine-tenths of the built-up area is in square blocks with absolutely straight boulevards. The visitor who expected a city built in bits and pieces around a central medina or caravanserai must cross off this first cliche from the list of "Orientalisms" he brought with him on the trip. If he has not been back to the capital for ten years (or even five according to some) he can no longer find his way. New roads link the western part of the city to the northern quarters. Towering buildings have been erected right and left. Large stores, super-markets, self-service shops have been opened, public buildings, government departments and monuments have been built and an array of giant cranes show that Iran's development fever.

The taxi that picks you up at the modern Mehrabad International Airport first takes a stretch of motorway bordered by flower-decked bushes, goes around a spacious roundabout in the middle of which the remarkably beautiful Azadi (freedom) Tower has been erected then for kilometre after kilometre speeds along perfectly straight avenues crossing each other at right angles and punctuated at intersections by fountains, statues or flower-beds.

Views of Tehran

Golestan Palace and Rose Garden

The Golestan (Rose Garden) Palace was the Qajars' royal residence. Its garden is an oasis of coolness and silence in the heart of the city.

The main building, architecturally unpretentious, houses a museum with objects from the Qajar period in the overloaded and pompous style of last century.

In the Golestan garden, a one-story pavilion to the right and slightly behind the entrance, shelters one of the best organized museums in Tehran. Do not be discouraged by its scientific title. It contains about thirty show-cases presenting everything which makes up the basic originality of Iranian life in the various provinces of the country.

Shahid Motahhari (formerly Sepahsalar), a 19th-century Madrasah

It is termed indifferently Shahid Motahhari "Masjid" or "Madrasah". It is really a "madrasah", but like all Koranic schools, it includes a mosque.

The Imam Mosque integrated into the bazaar

The decision to build the mosque was taken in 1809 by Fath Ali Shah. It was completed in 1840 and is one of the new capital's oldest buildings. It provides a good initiation to traditional Iranian architecture.

If you go beyond the immense rectangle formed by the bazaar and its labyrinth of covered streets either to the left by Khayyam or to the right by Cyrus or Ray, you enter popular quarters, filled with a crowd of labourers, porters and watermelon vendors; traffic is slowed down by numerous carts, carrier-tricycles, handling the transport of goods between depots and workshops engaged in mysterious activities.

Golestan Palace (19th century), Motahhari (Sepahsalar) Mosque, 19th cent., aerial view of Tehran's urban highways

Tehran became a capital in the 19th century. Its more ancient monuments bear the marks of that period when everywhere in the world, taste had degenerated. Furthermore, its rapid growth explains the proliferation of houses without any style, fortunately laid out in square blocks, but anonymous, without harmony, grey, with never a flower on their window-sills. The baroque and pretentious appearance of certain facades, particularly banks, built twenty or thirty years ago, do nothing to improve the city's appearance.

Old Tehran, Imam Mosque and old quarter in south of Tehran

Contemporary Arts Museum

Daring modern buildings, erected during the past few years, give, despite their frequently dry architecture, an impression of what Tehran's beauty will be in the year 2000. The Islamic Parliament, the Vahdat Hall, the City Theatre with its circular shape recalling that of Mongol towers, even the Esteqlal and Evin Hotel foreshadow the city of the future, and of course the Azadi Tower which dominates them all.

Modern Tehran: Mellat Park, City Theatre, urban highway

The capital of a veritable boom town undergoing intense activity, continues to expand according to a rational plan in a checkered pattern. Modern buildings rise up beside 19th century houses.

Modern Tehran: Keshavarz Blvd., Mellat Park, Vali-e Asr Square, Horr Square, south of Tehran

213

Three thousand years of history at the Archaeological Museum

Iranians call the Archaeological Museum "Iran Bastan". It looks out onto a small square off Imam Khomeini Avenue, about 100 metres from the Central Post Office. A guide-book is available in several languages. The displays were rearranged in 1971. Wallsigns are in French, which is exceptional, probably because French archaeologist Andre Godard was the initiator of the museum. Seen from the outside, the building gives no indication whatsoever of the wealth of art treasures it contains.

Iranologists find here an inexhaustible source of study. Objects uncovered during recent excavations are to be found side by side with objects representing the great periods of history and pre-history.

In about two hours, the tourist gets a comprehensive view of Iranian art throughout the ages: the ground floor covers Antiquity up to and including the Sassanian period, the first floor is devoted to the Islamic period. But most visitors come to admire a few much-photographed items which have become famous all over the world: Sialk Potteries with astonishingly "modern" stylized decorations (11th-6th century B.C.); terracotta animals of the same period from the Caspian and Azerbaijan regions, several famous Lorestan bronzes (8th century B.C.); the famous delicately chiselled Marlik gold tankard with its decor of winged rams (10th century B.C.). Gold and silver chest-plates, cups and dishes show how long the tradition of rich metal craft was kept up throughout the centuries.

Visitors who do not have time to go to Persepolis or Susa will find in the Iran Bastan (Archaeological) Museum significant vestiges of Achaemenian decorations: enamelled brick panels, bull head shaped column capitals, gold plates engraved with royal decorations in three languages (ancient Persian, Babylonian, Elamite) and so on.

Achaemenian rhyton and golden plaque found in the foundation of Apadana Palace at Persepolis, Tehran Museum

214

Tehran is pleasant. It derives its originality from its dry climate, always cool in the evening, its pure sky, the nearness of the mountains, its numerous parks and gardens where flowers blossom throughout the year, the alleys of young plane-trees in the avenues or even smaller streets, the water which runs down from the upper city along deep and wide gutters which look like small rivers unless it is stored in canals on a central terrace before being distributed to pools and fountains on squares and roundabouts. All this contributes to the pleasure of a visit to Tehran.

In winter, the mountain hotels and ski-clubs at Shemshak, Shahrestanak and Dizin are full several days a week.

In all these places and in all circles of society, foreigners are warmly welcomed and listened to with consideration.

Mountains at the threshold of the city

A short excursion you should not fail to make on a Friday (the Iranians' Sunday) consists in a visit to Sarband, the road terminus north of Tajrish. The road runs alongside the Sa'dabad Palace, passes in front of the Darband hotel and ends at the entrance of a gorge on a small square where a bronze statue has been erected to honour Iranian mountaineers. In a much less ambitious venture, you can join the crowd of families setting off for a picnic and soon find yourself sitting in a chairlift. After a long aerial journey you reach a high valley.

Dozens of small houses with zinc roofs nestle among the bushes. Some are private dwellings, but most are coffee-houses. Mountain streams run among the tables. But everyone does not sit around a table, many of the customers prefer the ancient-style comfort of low divans covered with old carpets. Delicious "kababs" are peacefully consumed accompanied by boiling hot tea, Pepsi or Coca-Cola.

Excursion around Tehran: Darband, Eagle Village and Shemshak Skiing

The Alborz range separats the central plateau from the lush Caspian littoral,the only part of the country where the rainfall is plentiful. The highest peak in the country, MT. Damavand, is an extinct volcano covered in snow for most of the year.

Mount Damavand, the highest mountain in Iran, has for centuries attracted mountaineers, nomads and legends to its snow-covered slopes. The epic hero Feraidun wrestled and defeated the evil giant Zahhak, chaining him to a cave on the mountain peak. Villagers living near the base of the volcano still remark that Zahhak is straining to be free at the first signs of smoke or rumblings often heard deep within the mountain. On a clear day, the 18,550-foot cone is visible from Tehran, fifty miles away.

Flora in central Alborz

217

Nature of Shahrestanak on the road to Chalus

Yazd Province

Name:also Yazd, Yerdz. Situation and access: Provincial capital. Altitude 1,240 metres. 335 km S-E of Isfahan on a good road. 450 km N-E of Shiraz on a track. 370 km N-W of Kerman. Airport, regular Iran Air services to Tehran, Isfahan, Kerman. Railway.

In many respects, Yazd is a disconcerting city. From whichever direction you approach it, you have to drive for hours through a desert without any comparison with the solitude and sumptuous colours of the surroundings of Shiraz or Hamedan for example, and you suddenly come upon a town with endless avenues.

Cars, taxis, hundreds of bicycles and multi-purpose three-wheeled Vespas demonstrate the existence of a lively economic activity. Delivery boys come and go, bearing enormous bright-coloured skins of wool and silk. The covered streets ring to the clapping sound of the weaving looms, but in the suburbs, recently-built factories show that the era of craftsmen is waning. But manual crafts are still practised in the braziers', coppersmiths' and tinmen's quarter: they make sugar-loaf casts and enormous cauldrons as well as huge round-bellied cans placed in niches in the shadiest and coolest part of the vaulted streets and filled with drinking water for public consumption.

Like the large villages around it-such as fortified Aqda and Ardakan surrounded by a patch of greenery in the middle of the desert, — Yazd is built of cob and clay but everything looks very carefully maintained; even the smallest streets are stone-flagged.

The houses are surmounted by high turrets with openings oriented toward the dominant winds; they insure the ventilation of the lower parts of the house rather like air-vents on a ship.

Instead of traditional roughly squareshaped iwans, Yazd displays an original kind of architecture: very high and narrow portals surmounted by two endless twin minarets, the "Eiffel Towers of Islam" as the inhabitants call them. This type of architecture is illustrated by the Friday Mosque (the handsome flag-stones under its porch are engraved with several forms of writing), the Vaqt-o-Sa'at Mosque (which means "the time and the hour" since an astronomical clock is used there) and two or three Imamzadehs. Even the 19th century is represented by an enormous building, a sort of fronton also overhung by two giant turrets: it is the Tekiyeh-e Mir Chakhmaq which used to mark the entrance of a bazaar and served as a background for theatre performances, relating the "Passion" of Hosain the Third Imam, assassinated at Karbala.

Jame' Mosque, Yazd

A historical city which regrets never having been a capital while so many now forgotten ones were, Yazd commemorates by unusual monuments the importance given it by scores of scientists and thinkers in past centuries.

It may be that the deep motivation of the city's healthy activity and its immoderate architecture is the secular competition which still exists in Iran between the Moslem majority and the Zoroastrian minority which is present and active everywhere.

The Zoroastrians devoted to the God of Light

During the Islamic conquest, (7th century), the last believers in the Zoroastrian faith fled to India (those among them at least who had sufficient means to take refuge abroad) and continued to celebrate their religion. They are now known as "Parsees". The others fled to the mountains around Yazd which then formed an impregnable refuge.

In practice, the rites of the Mazdaist religion are restricted to an initiation ceremony marking the age of responsibility, at about fifteen, for youths of both sexes, to regular offerings in front of the fire altar, to direct and personal communication with a single God and to handing over the dead to a brotherhood responsible for carrying them as quickly as possible into "Towers of Silence".

In these towers, eagles and vultures dispose of the bodies, thus avoiding that earth, water and fire, the divine elements be contaminated, the soul of the defunct person having already been welcomed by Ahura Mazda. Apart from the members of the brotherhood, nobody has ever been inside a Tower of Silence; no Zoroastrian has seen the inside consisting in tiers and a central well (but it is often possible by climbing a neighbouring hill to get a glimpse of torn clothes, the only vestiges of Mazdaist dead).

There are several Towers of Silence in the immediate vicinity of Yazd. Three of these are on top of three hills less than a kilometre out of the city. Another one, although completely isolated, is easily accessible to the left of the Yazd-Taft-Shiraz road (about 10 kilometres from Yazd). It dominates a magnificent desert and mountain site in which there are five or six Zoroastrian villages.

The Friday Mosque crowned by a pair of minarets, the highest in Persia, the portal's facade is decorated from top to bottom in dazzling tilework, predominantly blue in colour. Within there is a long arcaded court where, behind a deep-set south-east iwan, is a sanctuary chamber. This chamber, under a squat tiled dome, is exquisitely decorated with faience mosaic: it's tall finest of its kind in existence.

The mosque was largely rebuilt between 1324 and 1365, and is one of the outstanding 14th century buildings in Persia. The tile-work has recently been skillfully restored and a modern library built to house the mosque's valuable collection faience Mihrab, dated 1365, is one of the books and manuscripts.

Yazd, Jame' Mosque. The mosque basically achieved its present form under the Muzaffarids, but many elements of the decoration were added under the Timurids, including the facade of the main iwan.

Dowlatabad Garden

This a complex built according to the original Iranian architectural style and consists of a large garden and some buildings. Being watered by a *qanat*, until the very recent past it was used for the residence of the provincial governor. The most impressive part of the complex are a 33- meter high *bad-gir* (wind tower) on the roof and a water stream in the interior. The air was conducted into the interior and cooled through the action of the flowing water. Lattice doors and windows with stained glass patters impart a pleasing sight to the complex.

Pavilion of Dowlatabad Garden, 9th century, traditional tea-house, Yazd, old district

223

Yazd, bazaar entrance, 19th century. This incredibly imposing bazaar entrance was an excuse for a magnificent display of ostentation. The bazaar itself is comparatively small, but the entrance is undoubtedly the grandest in Iran. The twin minarets rival those of the Jame' mosque, while the entire facade is decorated with glazed tiles and plaster stalactite vaulting. The wooden framework is decorated and carried during the procession for the mourning for Imam Hosain.

Yazd bazaar and traditional trades.

This is Yazd's "fire temple". The initiates meet there, but nobody apart from the Grand Priest, a descendant of the Magi, reciting the Avesta, has access to the Saint of Saints where for the past 3000 years a fire burns in a brazen vessel, the symbol of the God of Light according to Zoroaster.

These " towers of silence " overlook an impressive desert and mountain landscape where the last worshippers of the Ahura Mazda faith dwell.

Yazd, Dowlatabad garden, and its famous louvre (wind tower)
  The heat is blistering in the south, on the edge of the Great Desert. High chimneys acting as air-vents bring some comfort to these dwellings.

Yazd, wind-tower. These wind-towers are a major architectural feature of southern Iran and the Gulf area generally, and are designed to catch any wind

and funnel it to the room below. This method is very effective and successfully lowers the temperature by several degrees.

Enormous domes starting at ground level and also surmounted by airvents act as protective roofs for deep water-tanks six, eight or ten metres below street level, which are reached by staircases. These buildings are so clean and well cared for that they look as if they were built yesterday.

Taft (25 km S-W of Yazd on the Shiraz road) has a Zoroastrian majority which has settled on the banks of the torrent which is often not dry and whose bed is used as a road. Upstream, beautiful gorges are accessible by car over a distance of several miles.

Because of its hugs size and wide climatic range, Iran offers a spectacular variety of scenery. Much of the central part of the country is sand and salt desert, including some of the most inhospitable terrains to be found anywhere in the world, but around these deserts are fertile plains watered by two large mountain ranges, the Alborz in the north and the Zagros in the south-west.

ایرانیان سرزمین افسانه‌ای

گزیده‌ای از آثار عکاسان ایران

با مقدمه‌ای از: دکتر جابر غناصری

طرح و اجرا: جواد یساولی

ایران سرزمین افسانه ای

آثار عکاسان ایرانی

گردآورنده: جواد یساولی

تصویر جلد: محمد کوچکپور کپورچالی

تفکیک رنگ: مگاپس، فرایند گویا

لیتوگرافی: نقش آفرین

نقشه : هوشنگ نعمتی ، حسین ستاری

چاپ هفتم بازنگری مجدد: ۱۳۷۹

چاپ: شادرنگ

تیراژ : ۴۰۰۰ جلد

ناشر: انتشارات یساولی

تهران : نرسیده به میدان انقلاب، بازارچه کتاب – تلفن: ۶۴۶۱۰۰۳ فاکس : ۶۴۱۱۹۱۳

تهران : خیابان کریم خان، نبش خردمند، پلاک ۸۰ – تلفن ۸۳۰۴۱۵ نمابر: ۸۸۳۲۰۳۸

آدرس اینترنت: www.yassavoliran.com

شابک : ۰-۰۱۶-۳۰۶-۹۶۴

یساولی، جواد ، ۱۳۲۳-   ، گردآورنده.
ایران سرزمین افسانه ای: گزیده ای از آثار عکاسان ایرانی/ با مقدمه ای از جابرعناصری؛
طرح و اجرا جواد یساولی؛ مترجم شاکه هاراتونیان.— تهران : یساولی / ۱۳۷۹.
ج، ۲۴۸ ص : مصور (تمام رنگی).

ISBN 964-306-016-0

فهرستنویسی بر اساس اطلاعات فیپا.
ص. ع. به انگلیسی:
Javad Yassavoli . The
fabulous land of Iran: colourful and vigorous folklore.
فارسی – انگلیسی.
آثاری از عکاسان ایرانی
چاپ هفتم
۱. عکسها -- ایران. ۲. عکاسان -- ایران. الف. عناصری، جابر، ۱۳۲۴-   ، مقدمه نویس.
ب. هاراتونیان، شاکه ، مترجم. ج. عنوان. د. عنوان: گزیده ای از آثار عکاسان ایرانی.

۹۲الف ۵ ی / TR۶۵۴   ۷۷۹/۹۹۵۵
                                    ۷۷۹/۹۹۵۵
                        [۹۵۵/۰۰۲۲۲]
۱۳۷۹   [DSR ۷۸]
کتابخانه ملی ایران   ۷۹-۵۸۸۵م

آثار عکاسان:

نیکل فریدنی

افشین بختیار

محمود شهرابی

بهرام عابدینی

غلامحسین عرب

محمدرضا بهارناز

سعید محمودی ازناوه

محمد کوچکپور کپور چالی

علی متین

حمیدرضا حسین زاده

اصغر آدمی

عبدالله کیوانی

عبدالخالق طاهری

افشین علیزاده

اسد نقشبندی

یدالله ولی زاده

مسعود زنده روح کرمانی

حسین رحمانی

فاطمه تعمیدی

یادداشتهای پراکنده ناشر

هرگز خود را در آن مرتبت نه پنداشته ام که در محضر اساتید جسارت ورزیده و فرس چوبین قلمم را در جولانگاه فرهنگ و ادب بجولان در آورم و سیاه مشقم را در جوار مرقع زرین آنان ارائه نمایم، لکن رسم دیرین ناشرین مبنی بر نگاشتن سطوری چند در بیان انگیزه شان از اثری که نسبت به نشر آن همت گماشته اند، بهانه ای بوده است تا با تمسک بدان سطوری چند را مسوده نمایم.

بلحاظ حرفه پدری از کودکی با کتب مصوری در ارتباط با ایران آشنا بوده ام و همواره چاپ کتابی در این باره ذهنم را بخود مشغول داشته و آرزوی دیرینه ام بوده است. این آرزو بلحاظ عوامل عدیده سالها جامهٔ عمل نپوشید. استفاده از آثار عکاسان تلاشگر و جوان و گسیل آنان به مناطق مختلف اندیشه ای بود که بدان راه یافتم و در تهیه این دفتر از آنان استعانت طلبیدم. پاسخ این طلب حاصلش کتابیست که آنرا مشاهده می کنید.

باید صادقانه اعتراف کنم علیرغم صفحات عدیده و تصاویر متعدد در ارائه بخش کوچکی از هزاران جلوه این سرزمین کهنسال نیز ناتوان مانده ام. تنوع فرهنگها و گونه های متفاوت طبیعت در سرزمینی که به جرأت می توان آنرا هفت اقلیم در یک اقلیم خواند، آنقدر گسترده است که در خیال هم نمی گنجد و ارائه بخش مختصری از آن نه در یک کتاب که در دهها کتاب نیز ممکن نیست و نه تنها افرادی نظیر حقیر که چندین سازمان دولتی نیز قادر نخواهند بود بخش مختصری از آنرا بتصویر درآورند.

در تدوین این کتاب گزینش تصاویر بمانند مضراب هایی بوده است که با ترنم آن سعی شده ویژگیهای اقلیمی و فرهنگ و هنر مردم یک منطقه در گوش جان بیننده دمیده شود.

در اولین جلسه از کلاس درس آنهنگام که برای مدت قلیلی در دیار فرنگ رحل اقامت افکنده بودم یک دانشجوی انگلیسی در حالیکه به میزم نزدیک میشد پرسید، ایرانی هستید؟ و بدون آنکه منتظر جوابم بماند به شعف گفت "من ایران را دیده ام، چه سرزمین زیبایی است". و سپس به توصیف اماکنی پرداخت که از آنها دیدن کرده بود. ابنیه و آثاری که من در مدت ۲۸ سالی که در آن هنگام از سنم می گذشت، نتوانسته بودم حتی عکس آنها را ببینم ، "قلعه الموت را دیده اید!؟" چقدر جالب است، و من شرمنده از خویش تنها با تکان سر و تبسمی دروغین حرفش را تصدیق می کردم، یادم می آید در مدت اقامتم کوتاهم در آنجا حتی آسیاب خرابه های محل اقامتم را نیز نگذاشته بودم از نگاهم بگریزد، اما در زادگاهم جز در محیطی چند کیلو متری از محل کارم فراتر نرفته بودم. نمی دانم چرا یکباره به عنوان مقاله ای افتادم که هیچگاه نخواندمش؛ "فرزند ایرانی از مادرش بی اطلاع است".

وقتی جهت تدوین کتابی با عکاسی معتبر از کشورمان، آثارش را مشاهده میکردم در بسیاری از موارد انگشت حیرت گزیدم که آیا آنچه را که می بینم جلوه هایی از سرزمینی است که در آن زندگی می کنم! و غبطه می خوردم بر او که اینها را در واقعیت و نه در رویا دیده و با فشار بر شاتر دوربین آنها را بثبت رسانده است.

متأسفانه صرف نظر از تورهای داخلی که اخیراً فعالیتشان را گسترده کرده اند کوششهای در خور توجــه در جــهت شناساندن زوایای ناشناخته طبیعی و اجتماعی کشورمان صورت نگرفته است و سازمانها و رسانه هــای تصویــری نــیز کمتر بدین مهم پرداخته اند و گاه در ارائه صحیح آن نیز ناتوان مانده اند. مصداق عدم شـناخت صحیـح از فرهنـگ و فولکلور ملی در تهیه سریالهای تلویزیونی و فیلمها مشهودتر است. در موارد بسیاری قبای سپید و پیچه مردان تربت جام را بر قامت رشید مردان بختیاری پوشانده اند و لباس محلی زنان تالش را تن پوش عشایر فارس و قشقایی قرار داده اند و حرکات رقص موزون مردان کُرد را در اجراء مراسم برای ایلاتی هزاران کیلومتر دورتر بکار گرفتــه انــد. بــا توجه به اینگونه کاستی ها و با عدم شناخت صحیح از قابلیت های اقلیمی و فرهنگهای متنــوع ایـن سرزمین پـهناور چگونه خواهیم توانست در معرفی آن به دیگران موفق باشیم؟

بسیاری از شهرهای اروپا دارای بافتی یکسانند. گاه مرز چندین کشور را بدون اینکه تغییری در ساختار معمــاری و معیشت مردم آن مشهود باشد درمی نوردید. آنچه که غربیان را مجذوب و راغب بدیدن این سرزمین نمــوده، تنوعــی است که در فاصله ای نه چندان دور از یک شهر به شهر دیگر پدید میآید. لذا چنانچه در نگهداری ویژگیهای خاص هر منطقه نکوشیم و در مقابل زودن و تغییر شکل آنها به شیوه غربی بی اعتنا بمانیم، در آینده ای نه چندان دور نشــانی از آنچه که آنرا شناسنامه و هویت یک منطقه می دانیم، نخواهیم یــافت و در نتیجــه دیــدار شـهرهایی بسـبک و شـیوه شهرهای غربی جذابیتی را برای بازدید کننده غربی بهمراه نخواهد داشت.

چندی پیش آرشیتکتی فرانسوی ایرانی تبار با تأسف از تخریب بافت قدیمی و خانــه هــای روسـتایی ابرقــو یــاد می کرد و قصد داشت گروهی را جهت تهیه طرحی از بافت قدیمی شهر، قبل از آنکه خانه های سـیمانی و تــیر آهنــی همچون غده ای سرطانی نسوج شهر را ببلعند، به منطقه گسیل نماید. در اینجا یکباره شعری از آقــای علــی موسـوی گرمارودی بیادم آمد و بدرستی نمی دانم آیا اینجا آن شعر جایگاهی دارد یا خیر.

های ای مردم! تبه شد عمرهاتان، های!

بار بر بندید و بگریزید: سوی رود و آب: سوی باغ و راغ

سوی آنجایی که مردم از میان کشتزارانی که می کارند نان گرم می روید

جانتان در آهن آجین شهرتان فرسود

***

گفته بودم بار بربندید؛ گفتم و اینک پشیمانم:

ترسم آنجا هم شما تا پای بگشایید؛

هر چه آبادی و آزادی ست، با پلیدیهای شهریتان بیالایید!

مطالب انگلیسی کتاب خلاصه ایست از کتبی که در صفحات اولیه متن انگلیسی بذکر آنها اقدام گردیده است وحقیر بــا بازخوانی و تلخیص آنها مطلب در خور هر تصویر را فراهم آورده ام.

در این چاپ با توجه به گذشت زمانی بالغ بر ۷ سال نیاز تجدید نظر در تصاویر کتاب بسیار محسوس می نمود، لذا در این چاپ نسبت به بخش وسیعی از تصاویر چه بلحاظ کیفی و چه بلحاظ تغییرات ساختاری بناها تجدید نظر شد.

از آنجا که خود را ملزم به درج نام عکاسان هر تصویر میدانسته ام لذا در پایان فهرستی از تصاویر هر یک از افراد آمده است.

بدیهی است بدون لطف بیدریغ آقای محمود شهرابی و افشین بختیار کـه قسمت اعظم عکسـها را در اختیـارم نهادند و علاقمندی دیگر عکاسان، آقایان بهرام عابدینی، غلام حسـین عـرب، محمـد رضا بهار نـاز، علی متیـن، سعید محمودی ازناوه، محمد کوچکپورکپور چالی، حمیدرضا حسین زاده ، مسعود زنده روح کرمانی، عبدالله کیوانـی، عبدالخالق طاهری، افشین علیزاده، اسد نقشبندی، یدالله ولی زاده، اصغرآدمی، حسین رحمانی، فاطمه تعمیـدی کـه تصاویرشان زینت بخش این مجموعه گردیده است کار انجام نمی پذیرفت. همین طور سپاسـگزاری از آقـای نیکـل فریدنی که تصویر کوهپایه دماوند در ابتدای کتاب و نقش خسرو پرویز در طاق بستان و تصویر غـار شـاهپور از آن اوست . امیدوارم این دوستان همین کتاب را مظهر سپاس و قدردانی و ستایش این دوستدار به شمار آورند.

در پیشبرد امور چاپ کتاب و کارهای اجرایی خود را مدیون بسیاری، از افراد میدانم. توجـه شـایانی کـه مسئولین مجتمع الکترونیک و گرافیک مگاپس، فرآیند گویا، نقش آفرین از آغاز نسبت به این کتاب مبذول داشـتند و همکـاری مؤثر آقایان تابانفر، رسایی، مرحوم سلطان محمدی، توکلی، کوهرنگی، محمد خانی، میر شمس، افضلی و سر کار خانم کامبوریان و سر کار خانم مگی موجب کمال تشکر است.لطف آقای حمید رضا سناجیان که با بردباری کج سلیقگی این حقیر را تحمل کردند و از آغاز حروفچینی کتاب همکاری صمیمانه ای را مبـذول داشـتند در خـور توجـه و قـدر دانـی است.سپاس ستایش انگیز خود را نیز به دوست ارجمند جناب دکتر جابر عناصری استاد دانشگاه که متن مقدمه به قلم شیوای ایشان نگـارش یافته تقدیم میدارم. از آقای هوشنگ نعمتی برای تهیه نقشه جغرافیایی و سرکار خـانم سـونیا رضا پورجهت ترجمه تطبیقی زیر نویس عکسها و تصحیح متن سپاسگزارم. در امور چاپ کوشش کار سـاز مدیریـت چاپخانه و مسئولین فنی و دیگر همکارانشان شایسته قدر دانی است.

جوادیساولی

مقدمه

گفت معـشوقــه به عاشــق کـأی فـتی

تـو به غـربـت دیـده ای بـس شهرهـا

پس کدامیـن شهر از آنها خوشتر است؟

گفت: آن شـــهری کـه کوی دلـبر است

ایران، دیار صفا و سرزمین مردان اهل وفا و زنان سخت کوش وهـنرمندان همیشـه در کوشـش و پویـش اسـت. خاستگاه عارفان و عاشقان و دردانه ای از مشرق زمین و سرزمین افسانه ای از شرق پر رمـز و راز و مـأمن شـاعران غزلخوان و خطّهٔ معماران شیوا پنجه و نقّاشان و خطّاطان صاحب ملاحت و نازش قلم و نقّالان شـیرین سـخن و آینه کاران آینه بند حجلهٔ نو عروسان و گچکاران گچبر آراینده رف زرنگار خانه ها و کاشانه هاست. ایران، در آغوش گیرندهٔ کاروانسراها و رباط های محلّ اطراق و آرامباش کاروانیان صاحب امتعهٔ گوناگون از حریر و پرند و دارنده خورجین های پر از زمرّد و یاقوت و حاملان پیام فرهنگی از شرق اقصی تا غرب پر غوغاست. زمانی شاهراه ابریشم از سـینهٔ او مـی گذشت و سنگفرش های راه های ارتباطی از چین و ماچین و ختن تا بیزانس، به میادین عرضهٔ متاع در قلب ایران ختم می شد و شکوفایی فرهنگی مشرق زمین، چشم اهل فرنگستان را خیره می ساخت. سوق هـا محـلّ فحـص و بحـث عالمان بود و.... امروز نیز تنوع فرهنگی و تعدّد جوامع از شرق ایران و از میان عشایر تیمانی و تیموری و جمشـیدی و فیروز کوهی تا کوچندگان مامِش و زرزا در غرب ایران و گالش ها و تالش های آرمیده بر سینه سـبز و مخمل نشـان چمنزارهای شمال و زندگی بلمرانان خلیج فارس در حاشیه برکه های خوش ساخت و پر نقش و نگار جملگی گشـاینده پردهٔ هزار رنگ عجب در قلمرو شناخت آداب و رسوم و آیین های بومی و محلّی وملّی و... است. از آلاداغ تـا سـهند و سبلان و زاگرس و البرز و الوند و دنا و کلاهخود کافوری رنگ آتش فشان تفتان، همگی دایه مـهربان روستانشـینان و شهرنشینان و کوچندگان رمه گردان است.

یادمان باشد که ایرانیان در طی زمان پناهگاهی نمی جستند مگر آنکـه سـقف و دیـوار و ازار و کنـگره و پیشـانی ساختمان را به نقوش زیبا و به آرایند. نقش رستم سینه ستبر را بر سر در دروازه ها به مردانگی مجسّم مـی نمودنـد و کاسهٔ زانوی او را بر قلب دیو سفید استوار می کردند و دمار از روزگار آن ناپاک و کژخو در مـی آوردنـد. رسـتم سـردر گرمابه ها نیز تماشایی می نمود. همه بیاری نقش بود و قلم نقاش در تک و پو. به گرمابه ها که قدم مـی گذاشتـند دو بیت شعر نغز را به خطّ جلی نگاشته می یافتند که آری:

هر که دارد امانتی موجود   به سپارد به بنده وقت ورود

نسپارد اگر شود مفـقـود   بنده مسئول آن نخواهـم بود

طاق های ضربی به قدرت و استحکام، نشانی از گنبد دوّار بودند و از دیدگاه زیبایی شناسی معماران با بهرگیری از علم استحسان، صفا و وفای اهل زیر گنبد را نشان می دادند. چنین است که گلگشت و تماشا در دیار مدام بهار ایران، ره توشه ای از عشق و ذوق می طلبد تا پاتاوه ای از همّت بر پاهایمان بربندیم و بـا چاووشـان سـفرهای زیـارتی و سیاحتی همگام گردیم و رهسپار مناطق طرفه و غریبه شویم و خنگ قلم را در صد میدان تماشا به دوانیم و بر توسـن خیال شهپر عاطفه تقدیم کنیم و فریاد برآوریم که:

هر دم از روی تو نقشی زَنَدَم راه خیال   تو چه دانی که در این پرده چه ها می بینم

امّا در این دیدار نه خیال که عین واقع است و همباشی با اهل ولایات، غنیمت است و موجب اشتیاق.

با هم، همقدم شویم و درحریم مقدّس ایران زمین، کهن شـهری از مشـرق و گوهـری از خـاوران و دردانـه ای از بیادگار مانده از روزگار باستان، به سیر و سیاحت بپردازیم:

اینک بر هودج کاروانیان مشتاق زیارت حرم حضرت ثامن الائمه غریب الغربا امام رضا (ع) اطراق می کنیم و پـرده کجاوه را به یکسو می زنیم تا به بانک بشارت چاووشان، قبه طلایی آرامگاه ضامن آهو را بنگریم و پرنده بیقـرار دل را روانه صحن و سرای آن حضرت نماییم تا با کبوتران محرم حـرم، در آسمان خراسان سـرزمین آفتـاب تابـان بـال بگشاید. و ما از بـاب تهیّهٔ سـوغاتی از عطـر و زعفـران و شـاخ نبـات، بـازار مشـهد را زیـر پـا بگذاریـم و عرقچین های زیبا را با طرح های سوزن دوزی شده، در برابر دیدگان ببینیم و فیروزه های بر گرفتـه از کـان و معـدن دیار نیشابور را نگین انگشتری سازیم و مهر و تسبیح و سجّاده، همگی آراسته به عطر ایمان را در خورجین سفر قـرار دهیم و سپس، بار سفر بربندیم و به دشت ترکمن آنجا که گل میخ های آلاچیق های ترکمن هـا اسـتوار گشتـه قـدم بگذاریم. گنبد کاووس را تماشا کنیم و بر لب جویی به نشینیم و گذر عمر را دریابیم و فاتحه ای از بـهر اهـل قبـور در گورستان ترکمن ها بخوانیم و سنگ مزارهای نقشین را با طرح و برش خاصّی بنگریم که شاخ پیچ در پیچ قـوچ و بـز پیشاهنگ گله را عیان می سازند. آری در این گلگشت و تماشاست که پنجشنبه بازار آق قلا در ترکمن صحرا دیـدگان

ما را از نظاره سجّاده های نماز به خیرگی می کشاند. آنجا که به خون سرانگشتان بافندگان، طفلان نقش باسیل خُون در آمیخته اند و هر نقشی به سوزن مژگان خونپالای چشمان هنرمندان جان گرفته و قیامت قامت نقش، عیار کار رسّام و نقشه خوان قالب و قالیچه گشته است.

هلا ای امیر کاروان، حال بلد راه ما باش و ما را به آرامگاه خیّام در نیشابور راهنمایی کـن تـا بـه مـزار آن شـاعر شوریده، سخن از دهر و روزگار و گذر عمر بر زبان بیاوریم و سپس در الله آباد یزد، کاشی های منقـوش را در حاشـیه درها با گل میخ های زیبا و کوبه های پر رمز و راز تماشا کنیم و آنگاه از مأذنهٔ مسجد سمنان گلبانگ محمدی بشنویم و رستم – آن دلاور دوران – را جان ستان دیو سفید بشناسیم و نقش هماورد خوانی او و کوبیدن دیو سفید بر خاک سـرد آوردگاه را بر سر در دروازه سمنان شاهد باشیم و دستان بر پیشانی سایه بان سازیم و از دور دستها حکیـم تـوس را نگران چالش شهسواران عرصه پیکار در جهان اسطوره ها ببینیم که نگاه تمثال حکیم، بر نقش پیکره های نقر شده بر دیوار موزه توس گره خورده و همو بارگاه سخن را به رفعت و عزّت نگهبان گشته و معمار بارگاه سخن خوانـده شـده است. حال گوش می سپاریم و آوای نقاره زنان صحن حضرتی در مشهد را به گوش جان می شـنویم. سپس اسـب راهوار پژوهش را از شرق به جنگل های سر سبز شمال می داونیم و پا در رکاب سفر می گذاریم و کرت های چـایی و خانه هایی با سقف سفالی را می نگریم و به آوای حزین بلمرانان ساحل خزر پاسخ می دهیم که آری:

شب تاریک و بیم موج و گردابی چنین هایل　　　　　　　کجا دانند حال ما سبکباران ساحل ها

غم آواز این صیّادان به کولاک دریا می پیوندد و دردانه های ترانه هایشان، رامش و خیزش و پویش موج ها را رقم می زند.

در عالم دیدار، از جمعه بازار دشت گرگان تا شنبه بازار دیار سر سبز شـمال، یـک صـد ارس راه بیـش نیسـت و ترانه های بلمرانان و آوای دلنشین شالیکاران درهم می آمیزد. تـور بافـان، حلقـهٔ ریـز تـور صیـد را گره در گره بـهم می بافند.

با هم به همراه عکاس هنرمند، به بندر انزلی می رسیم و مرداب رابا نیلوفرهای آبی و مرغابی ها و غازهای وحشـی در برابر دیدگان می یابیم و چشمان فرو می بندیم تا اسارت ماهیان بی قرار را در تور صید صیّاد شاهد نباشیم و آنگاه چشم بگشاییم و مناظر طبیعی حاشیه جنگل در استان گیلان و استان مازندران را تحسین کنیم و حـظّ بصر بـبریم و میهمان سفرهٔ چهل تکّهٔ گالش ها و تالش های اهل دل شویم و در مراسم شادمانی گیلک ها شرکت نماییم و به کاسه ای از شیر داغ بر گرفته از دستان شبانان صاحب گاوسرا تن خسته را به آرامش بکشانیم و با نوروزی خوانان آن دیـار همصدا گردیم و نوروز سلطان و نو بهار خجسته را تبریک بگوییم و مراسم «تکم گردانی» را نظاره کنیم کـه نـوروزی

خوانان با چرخاندن عروسکی موسوم به «تکه» یا «تکا» به نوبهار خوانی، اشتیاق رسیدن به بهار را صـد چنـدان مـی سازند.

هشیار باشیم که ماسوله این کهن شهر عتیقه در بهار خواب های خانه هـایش گل پامچـال کاشـته و پنجـر هـای مشبک چوبین خانه ها در آن شهر دلربا، شمسه هایی زیبا با اشکال دلنشین دارند.

در سوی دیگر، کوچه های آشتی کنان حاشیه کویر با گذرگاه های باریک و سقف طاق ضربی،آوای هلهله و هروَلـه سوگواران و حمل علم و کتل و نخل عزاداری از برای حضرت سید الشهدا علیه السلام، جملگی متجلّـی در قـاب آینـهٔ دوربین عکّاس و گره قالی با گره چینی در کاشی که همباشی و همراهی، نمایندهٔ ذوق هنرمندان عامی است. هنرمندانی که بادگیرها و آس بادها و دژها و برج و باروها را استوار ساخته و کنگره هایی بر دور حصار شهرها کشیده اند. دسـتان مریزاد که لعل و فیروزه و یاقوت نیشابور و سایر دیارها را به محک زده و پنجره های ارسـی را بـا کلـون هـای حـافظ درهای چوبی، به زیبا وجهی آماده کرده و نام شفاخانه را به روی کاشی نگاشته و ترنج و شمشاد را به ذوق و خیـال از باغ و بوستان بر گرفته و در قالب نقش بر سینه صحن و سرای مساجد به نمایش درآورده اند. در گوشه گوشـهٔ ایـران عزیز، کاروانسراها محلّ اطراق کاروانیان گشته و گرمابه ها با نقش و نگار سردرها و «عمل» استاد کـاران، از سـلطان محمّد معمار یزدی گرفته تا استادان دیگر- که از دیر گاه آراینده رف چینی خانهٔ دل اهل نظر بوده انـد، آذیـن یافتـه و موقوفاتی از افراد خیّر و نیکوکار همچون گنجعلی خان را در کرمان به مرمّت و همت بر پای نگهداشته و حمّام گنجعلی خانی کرمان را شهره آفاق نموده اند. باغ و راغ و سرو و شمشاد و عمارت کهنه های میان گنبد و سقف وازار سـاختمان همچون گنبد گبری- دوره سلجوقی- تمثالی از گنبد دَوار آسمان است و مقبرهٔ شاه نعمت ا... ولی آن سـر سـپاه مـولا علی (ع) به ملاحت قلم خطّاط و به همت استاد کاشیکار، به یاهو ویا من هوی شیدایان بارگاه الهی مزیَن گشته و آوای قلندران در زیر گنبد پیچیده که:

پس قدم مردانه در راه خدا باید زدن.

باغ ارم شیراز، گوشه ای از پردیس برین را مجسّم می سازد و کاشیکاریهای عمارات آن دیار بـرای اهـل تحقیـق زمینهٔ مطالعه در باب لباس شناسی و آداب و آیین های محلّی را فراهم می نماید. نقش و نگاری همچـون سـرباز دورهٔ قاجار و خدمتگزاران صحن و سرای دولتمندان و شمایل قلندری با مَن تشاء و کشکول و بـی نیـاز از هفـت اقلیـم و همآغوش مزار سعدی- آن مصلح الّدین خوش بیان- و همراه استاد میرزا عبدالرزاق نگارنده شرفنامهٔ کاشیکاران، همه نشان از شکوفایی هنر مردمی است. مسجد وکیل با ستون های برش دار و خداخانه (مسجد جامع عتیق) با مأذنـه ای درخور التفات، انگشت حیرت ما را بر دندان عجب می برد جمال کریم خـان - آن وکیـل الرعایـای برخاسـته از میـان

خاندان زند، موزهٔ فارس را می آراید. وکیلی که از مال دنیا به زیر اندازی بسنده کرده و تفنّن تفریحی بـه جـز تدخیـن نداشته است.

نمای آجر کاری ارک کریم خانی شیراز به ترکیب دلپسندی از نقوش هندسی، چشمان بینندگان و اهل نظر را خـیره می سازد.

امّا چه بگوییم از آرامکدهٔ حافظ آن دارندهٔ دردانه های غزل و دریا دلی غزلخوان برای تمام دوران. قسم بـه شـاخ نباتش که خاک مزارش توتیای چشمان زوّار شیدای دیدار با آن شاعر شوریده و دل بستن به تفالی از دیـوان خواجـه محمّد شیرازی، حافظ قرآن و آن کس که کتاب مقدّس قرآن را با چهارده تجوید می خوانده و سینه اش مأمن سوره ها مصحف قرآن همدم شبهای تارش بوده است، عین صواب است.

بازار شیراز، سوق و گذرگاه و شارع عامی است که عشایر با لباسهای الوان را در سینه جای می دهد و بیع و شرای نمد و شولا و پای افزار و... را به لطیفه گویی شیرازیان آشنا به عطر بهار نارنج همراه می سازد. کوچندگان رمـه گـردان نظیر: قشقایی، باصری، اینانلو، نفر، شیبانی و... بازار شیراز را محلّی طرفه می شناسند و جلیقه های پولک دوزی شده و کلاه نمدی دو گوش را از بازار وکیل ابتیاع می نمایند و دل به مهر و با دلی شاداب و رخی شادان، قافله ها را از کـوه و کتل اطراف شیراز عبور می دهند و کازرون را به زیر پا می گذارند و فاصلهٔ ییلاق و قشلاق و بالعکس را به طرفه العیـن می پیمایند. وقتی از کنار تخت جمشید عبور می کنند و لختی دربار انداز مجاور آن ساحت باستانی اطراق مـی نماینـد، لمحه ای درنگ می کنند و عظمت ایران را در تمام دوران به نظاره می نشینند. ضمن اینکه به عبرت به قصر و بـارگاه شاپور می نگرند و تصویری از فروهر را بر سر در معبدی تماشا می کنند و عطر برخاسته از آتشدان مقـدس را بـا دود اسفند و بخور و کندر استشمام می نمایند. برج خاموشان در مدّ نظر، از آیین های الهی - عبادی و مراسم خاکسپاری و دخمه بندی زرتشتیان نشانه ها در سینه دارند.

نیم نگاهی دیگر ما را به سوی اصفهان می کشاند که به حق نصف جهان شهرت یافتـه و صنایـع دسـتی آن دیـار نگین اقتدار هنرهای سنّتی ایران است و اصفهان محلّ تلاقی فرهنگها و اقوام مختلف از گرجـی هـا و ارامنـه و... کـه میهمان خطّهٔ اصفهان شدند و سپس به مهربانی در کنار اهل ایمان در اصفهان اطراق نمودنـد و خداخانـه ای از بـهر عبادت بر پا ساختند و کلیسایی زیبا آراستند و ناقوس کلیسا را به صدا در آوردند و همراه با گلبانگ محمّدی برخاسته از مأذنه ها از مهرو صفای عیسای مسیح یاد کردند و نقش و نگارهای چشم نـوازی از زنـدگی و شـهادت مسیح علیـه السلام را بر دیوارها جای دادند.

اصفهان با چایخانه های سنّتی، یاد آور فرهنگ دورهٔ صفوی و حاضر باش سفرا در این قهوه خانه هـا و محّل بـاز آفرینی مجالس سخنوری نقّالان است. سی و سه پل با منظرهٔ زیبایی از حاشیهٔ زاینده رود، سیّاحان اهـل گلگشـت و

تماشا را به وجد می آورد و نماز بی ریای دلبستگان به خدا در صحن و سرای مساجد اصفهان در قـاب آیینـهٔ دوربیـن عکّاس به عطر محبّت آمیخته می شود.

هنوز مدرسهٔ چهار باغ، به ندای طالبان علم صفا می یابد و فریاد گفتم، گفت آنان از بهر مباحثه و سیر جدالی کـلام، در گوش جان اهل نظر می پیچد.

وقتی قدم به صحن و سرای خانه های حاشیه نشینان کویر می گذاریم در می یابیم که ایران سـرزمینی اسـت بـا تنّوع فرهنگها و بر گرفتن حتّی یک نیم نگاه از تماشای شهرها و آبادیها و سیاه چادر کوچندگان پسندیده نمی باشـد. خانه هایی باهشتی و دالان و بیرونی و حوضخانه و اندرونی و تالار طنبی و بهار خواب ها، منظره ای زیبا در پیشگاه اهل نظر قرار می دهند.

فنّ و هنر و صنعت صنعتکاران و هنرمندان ذوالفنون ایرانی، همیشه ایام مورد تحسین خارجیان و سیاحّان موشکاف بوده است. ایرانیان به تکیه کلام و به ورد زبان و در قالب تمثیل و مثل می گویند: هر چیزی بـه فنّی اسـتوار اسـت و انسان باید فوت و فنّ کوزه گری و کاسه گری بداند.

تجلّی جمال و کمال در آثار هنری ایران را آشنا و بیگانه، ستوده اند و زندگی سنّتی ایرانیان را تحسین آمیز دانسـته اند. عطر و گلاب قمصر کاشان و زیرهٔ کرمان شهد و انگبین و عسل سبلان و آذربایجـان و قـالی کرمـان و کاشـان و فیروزهٔ نیشابور و گیوه های زیبایی از کردستان و سربندهایی از کرمانشـاهان و سـوزن دوزی و سـفال و کلپـورگان بلوچستان و منبّت و مینا و خاتم و اصفهان و شیراز، ارمغان و تحفهٔ طرفه ای برای اهل ینگی دنیاست. گلستان هـای سعدی عطر آگین قمصر فرسنگ در فرسنگ بوی عطر برخاسته از بـن کـاکل گل سـرخ محمّـدی و معطـر را درهـوا می پراکنند و لباس های محلّی ایرانیان اعجاب انگیز می نمـاینـد. نظـم و نظـام روش آبرسـانی از طریـق کاریزهـا و قنات ها، ظرافت اندیشهٔ ساکنان دریا زیبای ایران را عیان می نماید که چگونه قطرهٔ قطرهٔ آب را از سینهٔ زمین بیـرون می کشند و سر سبزی کرت ها و جالیزها و باغ و بوستان را سبب می شوند. هنرمندان چیره دست ایرانی، هـر دم کـه فرصتی می یابند، تصویری از رزم و بزم و سور و سوگ را بر سـینهٔ نیلـگون کاشـی و یـا رخ سـفید دیوارهـا مجسـم می سازند و چنان در نقش اندازی سقف خانه ها خبره می گردند که تو گویی آسمان آبی با ستارگانی از دبّ اکبر و دبّ اصغر و ستاره شامگاهی و ستارهٔ پگاه را بروی پردهٔ لاجوردی کاشی آشکار می کنند و پنجره هایی مشبّک را دریچه ای از جهان به سوی فضای بیکـران قـرار مـی دهنـد ودر طبقـه بنـدی بخـش هـای مختلـف عمـارت بـه اطـاق هـا و رف ها و صندوقخانه و .... ماهر می گردند.

خدا را امیر کاروان، مجالی تا بارو بنه از گرده اشتران خیال برگیریم و با ذوق و هوس، قدم در بازارها بگذاریم و در اصفهان پرده های قلمکار با نقش و نگارهای زیبا را تماشا کنیم که از خروج مختاربن ابو عبید ثقفی به عنوان خونخواه

حضرت حسین بن علی (ع) تا کوبیدن چوب حراج یوسف نبی (ع) در بازار مگارهٔ مصریان و سپس تماشای آن ملک سیما بر تخت و بارگاه عزیزی مصر ملاحت و به خصوص صحنهٔ داوری اخروی و روز محشر و گستره ظلم در ستم سرای کربلا- جملگی- نقش های چشمگیری است که بر این پرده ها بهار و وقار بخشیده اند.

همسفران، بیایید با هم همره شویم و بوی حنا و زعفران را در اسواق و بازارها استشمام کنیم و کلّه قندی و شاخ نباتی از بهر تقدیم به اهل شادمانی ابتیاع نماییم و در محفل شادی آنان حاضر شویم و در خوشباشی این شیدایان سهیم گردیم و نقل و نبات سور و سرور را بر دهان بگذاریم و کبوتر تیز پرواز خیال رابه کبوترخانه های اصفهان رها سازیم و با شگفتی به شیوهٔ معماری این کبوترخانه ها بنگریم که نقش زراعی- اقتصادی و کشاورزی و برکت دهی بر خاک- از طریق استفاده از این کبوترخانه ها- در خور تأمّل است. در گذشته های نه چندان دور، کبوتران پیک و نامه رسان در نهایت اوج و اعزاز موجب روشنایی دیدگان چشم انتظاران دریافت رقعه ای از همراهان و عزیزان سفر کرده بودند.

گامی دیگر برداریم و بر درگاه کاشان آن دارالقرار امام زاده شهید شهزاده سلطانعلی بن امام محمّد باقر علیه السّلام برسیم و بی ریا و به مهر و صفا، مزار امام زاده مظلوم را زیارت کنیم و زیارتنامه ای بخوانیم و در مشهد اردهال شاهد مراسم قالی شویان باشیم و درخانهٔ بروجردی ها پرندهٔ تیز بین چشمان را از رف خانه ای به صحن و سرای خانه ای و دالان و سقف و آب نما و گچبری کاشانه ای دیگر به پرواز در آوریم و دیدار از آرامگاه بابا افضل کاشانی صاحب مصنّفات را- به فاتحه ای- به جای بیاوریم ومحرم حرم اهل ذوق شویم که تختی در گوشه ای از حیاط منزل بر پا داشته و به مهر و وفا در کنار هم جوشانده ای از گل گاوزبان و بنفشه و سنبل طیب و .... را تهیّه کرده و صفاخانه ای آراسته اند و خشت و کاه وگل این خانه ها را به ملاط مهربانی، شیرازه بندی نموده اند.

اگر از خونابهٔ چشمان کاتبان مرکب بسازیم واز پردهٔ دل هزار هزار برگ کاغذ فراهم نماییم و در بلندای قیامت قامت ایران عزیز بر کتاب شناخت این دیار مقدّس مطلب بیفزاییم، به جرأت می توان گفت که این نوشته ها در خور خطه مقدس ایرانشهر، این آرامانشهر مشرق زمین نخواهد بود. سرزمین ایران، مردمک چشم خاوران را از یاد نبریم.

دکتر جابر عناصری

بیست و هشتم بهمن ماه یکهزار و سیصد و هفتاد و یک -تهران پ

Zanjan Province
Soltaniyeh (Khodabandeh)

Name: Formerly Soltaniyeh (The Imperial), Situation and access: Zanjan Province. Altitude 1,900 metres, 285 km N-W of Tehran, 365 km S-E of Tabriz, good road.

About halfway along the lengthy Tehran-Tabriz itinerary, where the road and railway line run across an unending plain bordered in the distance by unattractive mountains, you see to your left, at about 3 kilometres as the crow flies, an enormous cupola overlooking a small earthcoloured hamlet.

This forgotten site used to be the capital of the Mongol Soltans. Oljaitu, a recent convert to Shi'ism, got built there during his lifetime a grandiose mausoleum where he planned to put to rest the remains of the first Imams, Ali and his son Hosain the victims of the "Karbala tragedy". The plan was never implemented and the King himself was buried there upon his death in 1316.

The proportions of this tower with a hexagonal base, surmounted by a dome, are so harmonious that it is only when you are at the foot of its walls or inside it that you realize how gigantic a monument it is. The ogival cupola is 52 metres above ground level. (nearly as high as the 58 metres chancel of the Beauvais Cathedral in France which is the highest in the world). This architectural formula was used during subsequent period but not always so successfully. The ceramic decoration, now somewhat deteriorated, with the typically Mongol blue, black and white colour-scheme has an admirable effect. In order to get an overall impression it would be necessary to climb on the roof of the building.

Oljaitu Tomb, Soltaniyeh, Zanjan Province

232